GUATEMALA
OCCUPIED COUNTRY

GUATEMALA
OCCUPIED COUNTRY

by Eduardo Galeano

translated by
Cedric Belfrage

 NEW YORK AND LONDON

First published in Mexico under the title of
Guatemala: País Ocupado
© 1967 by Editorial Nuestro Tiempo, S.A.

English translation copyright © 1969
by Monthly Review Press
116 West 14th Street, New York, N.Y. 10011
33/37 Moreland Street, London, E.C. 1

Manufactured in the United States of America

Library of Congress Catalog Card Number: 68-8079

First printing

Contents

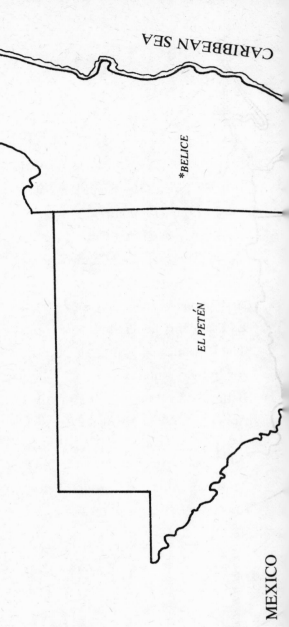

GUATEMALA:

showing departments
and principal cities

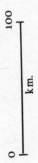

0   100

km.

*Territory claimed by Guatemala

CARIBBEAN SEA

*BELICE

EL PETÉN

MEXICO

Introduction to the English Edition

THIS IS THE HOUR of the spilling of blood. The blind violence of the colonels ravages the land. But the guerrilla aims at the head: the chief of the U.S. military mission in Guatemala falls. Julio César Méndez Montenegro's government expels North American priests. Are they spies or agents of imperialism? Could the President be jealous of them? No: he accuses these Catholic priests of the Maryknoll order of collaborating with guerrilleros. Father Thomas Melville tells the *National Catholic Reporter* in January 1968: "During the past 18 months three [right-wing terrorist] groups together have assassinated more than 2,800 intellectuals, students, labor leaders, and peasants who have in any way tried to organize and combat the ills of Guatemalan society." * Another expelled priest, Father Blase Bonpane, denounces this sick society in the *Washington Post* (February 4, 1968): "Of the 70,000 a year who die in Guatemala, 30,000 are children. Guatemala's child mortality rate is 40 times that of the United States." The misery is not written in the stars, not to be blamed on God. "In Guatemala," explains Father Bonpane, "the United States is standing militarily behind an oligarchy of two percent of the Guatemalan people who possess eighty percent of the land and resultant power."

THE MINISTER OF DEFENSE, who has real power in a country whose President is still a civilian but does not preside, says twice a month that the guerrillas are dead and buried. But the Guatemalan revolution does not seem to know about its fre-

* See Appendix III, p. 155.

quent demise, and painfully and tenaciously continues on its course.

Whence comes this force which has survived massive terror and military annihilation campaigns planned by Pentagon specialists, and which has been able to admit and overcome its own errors? The guerrilla movement is alive, the movement that is hinged to it is alive. That is its greatest victory—it exists, develops, wins victories and suffers defeats. *Its experiences have been a healthy diet, since it is still ready to embark on new ones. The lads who have taken up arms are not isolated, not something foreign to the reality of their field of action. They themselves are a consequence of the reality that challenges them.* Few in numbers as they are, they incarnate *collective* accusation of a system which starves the majority in favor of a minority. If such were not the case, the accusation could be easily covered up and explained away as the isolated anger of an aroused intellectual, or stifled lightheartedly as the protest of an isolated trade union on strike.

The guerrilla's persistence obliges the "constitutional" government to reveal how precarious and purely decorative it is. As violence sharpens race and class contradictions, the social, political, and military expression of those contradictions emerges with more terrible clarity. The right wing takes off its mask. This is its true face, the monstrous reality. Would it be better to live a lie, to disguise the tensions without overcoming them? The FAR (Rebel Armed Forces) guerrilleros and the Communist PGT (Guatemalan Labor Party) *also* voted for Méndez Montenegro as President. Both organizations expected the army to deny *power* to the victorious candidate, as in fact occurred. But they did not warn of the possibility— which also occurred—that the army might let him exercise innocuous and formal functions of government, thus giving the dictatorship "democratic" form.

The lightning of violence silhouettes the real nature not only of local oligarchic power, but of imperialism which proclaims reforms and trains armies to prevent them—the alien nature of the power structure, the essential hypocrisy of its methods of extortion and domination. The government can do nothing, but it does not have to; it need only let those act whose role is to act. Impotence is not neutrality, and if the army gives orders to the government, the Pentagon gives them to the army.

This little book is not only the result of direct contact with the guerrilleros in their mountain fastnesses and city hide-aways; above all it has grown out of direct, day-to-day aware-ness of the *causes* that explain the rebellion and justify it as historically necessary, and from contact with the *consequences* of the revolutionary process which, in turn, dialectically drive it ahead.

I BELIEVE that Guatemala is a key to Latin America. Why? From a geopolitical standpoint Guatemala might be seen as a colony condemned to perpetual non-fulfilment as a nation. The Caribbean is the *mare nostrum* of the Rome of our day, the second frontier of the United States. As part of a region vital to the security of the imperium, Guatemala must remain under its exclusive and undisputed hegemony. Mahan and Spykman have pointed out the imperial importance for North America's military defense of the countries around the Panama Canal. A thousand times it has been well said that the Cuban revolution cannot be reproduced as a new isolated phenome-non in Latin America; and if this is true for South America, how much more for the narrow Central American strip where the two oceans meet.

In a little Caribbean country so close to the enemy's jaws, how can a revolution that announces its socialist character hope to succeed and establish itself? A lone revolution, at this stage of the Latin American historical process, is a revolution marked for failure; much more so if it occurs in the suburbs of the U.S. The imperium will not permit any new intrusion into its "vital space."

Yet there is no reason why paralysis should result from realization of this strategic framework. The wind of revolution, as we know, blows where it lists. History is not simple, and chooses its direction heedless of the wishes, imaginings, or logic of the wisest prophets. Great social storms are not incubated in laboratories, nor are revolutionary processes played out in orderly fashion on chessboards. If they were, Czarist Russia would not have gone socialist; China would not have risen from its deep well of ignorance and misery to live thousands of years in two decades; nor would the Sierra Maestra *barbudos* have taken their delightful insanity to the point of creating in a flea-sized island, under imperialism's astounded, impotent and furious nose, the first socialist state in America.

In Guatemala the objective and subjective conditions of revolution are ripening faster than in the other Latin American countries. The process has a broader setting than the place where it is occurring. It is true, I think, that success can no longer crown any deeply revolutionary effort within the stagnant confines of a single Latin American country. The fight has to be waged on a continental scale, with an equally continental strategy, against an enemy who operates continentally. But should Guatemalan revolutionaries cross their arms waiting, for example, for Brazil—that huge potential powder-keg of Latin America—to awaken from its lethargy?

Who could be so stupid or so despicable as to want a small country to settle down impotently until continental conditions for revolution exist? By what right can we expect it to accept as "temporarily" inevitable the genocide that hunger and terror systematically commit upon its people, to resign itself to humiliation as a "passing evil"? Yes, the revolution will be Latin American or it will not be; but it is no less true that *the Latin-Americanization of the revolution will only result from the confluence and synchronization of diverse national revolutionary processes.*

Split by the frontiers that imperialism drew in order to rule them, the tormented lands south of the Rio Grande are united by a common historical origin, a common enemy, and the community of a destiny already glimpsed through blood and tears. Yet there are important differences between some Latin American countries and others, and thoughts and actions must be based on the realization that a single formula cannot apply to different situations. It would be a serious mistake to confuse Guatemala's largely Indian, peasant, and illiterate society with the cosmopolitan and predominantly middle-class society of Uruguay. Similarly, Colombia's peasant violence cannot be mechanically transposed to the reality of a country like Argentina, where giant Buenos Aires exercises the decisive weight.

From this point of view the Guatemalan revolutionary experience offers important keys for all Latin America. Not as a model to imitate, nor as a mirror which can exactly reflect the image of each of our countries, but as a source of great lessons painfully learned. In this sense, too, the young Guatemalans are spilling their blood for all of us. They die for us to the extent that, in clearing their revolutionary path at the cost of their lives, they help Latin Americans of every country to discover their own. Their fate is linked directly to that of all Latin America. It is a march against the clock. "The fight in each country, the struggle for the revolution in each country, is the best kind of solidarity for us," said *comandante* César Montes when I interviewed him in the mountains. If Latin America were to abandon Guatemala in the hour of great decisions, her heroism would also be her tragedy and her tragedy would be our guilt.

Just as Lenin vainly waited for the European proletariat to rise in the turbulent years after the storming of the Winter Palace, so Cuba, in its first revolutionary period, nursed the euphoric hope of continental insurrection. Six years after the Bolshevik victory the architect of Soviet power died; his revolution was still undefeated but still alone. In a few months the Cuban revolution will be ten years old. Flames lit by its sparks burn fiercely south of the Rio Grande, but no

other Latin American revolution has triumphed to end the
heroic Caribbean island's loneliness. In this half-century
history has run fast and the international relationship of
forces has changed. It would be obvious but irrelevant to point
out that the Cuban revolution, harassed by aggression and
blockade, has survived thanks to the strength of its own people
in arms as well as to the solidarity of the socialist world. Yet
in Latin America, Cuba goes her way alone. The natural
sources of sustenance for the Cuban revolution are or should
be Latin American. From the economic, geopolitical and
military standpoint the reasons for this are self-evident; from
the ideological standpoint they are less apparent but no less
real, related to the fact that this is the first socialist revolution
which speaks Spanish and shares a common origin and historical projection with all Latin America. At this point the
double achievement of Cuba, excluded from her natural setting, is extraordinarily impressive. In such conditions of continental isolation and dependence on supplies from across the
world, she has succeeded in carrying forward an independent
revolutionary line thought out in her own head on the basis
of her own reality and in saving herself from sectarianism and
dogmatism.

It seems to me that an impetuous desire to quicken the pace
of Latin America's revolutionary process—which for Cuba is
to some extent a desperate wish to end her solitude—and
justifiable indignation at the traitors and vacillators who delay
that process or condemn it to failure, explain Ernesto Guevara's great gesture of renunciation and commitment. Like the
last century's great heroes, Che gambled his life on the fate of
our disunited America's cause. Just as the life of this man from
Argentina incarnated Latin America's will to rebirth as a single
free nation, so his death incarnated the drama of its dismem-
berment and division. In dying he expressed better than anyone the urgencies of the Cuban revolution.

Every successful revolution tends to project its own image,
haloed with victory, as an international revolutionary model.

Cuba has been no exception to the rule, although she cannot honestly be accused of wanting to dominate Latin America's liberation movements. With its courageous rejection of the mental clichés which have petrified Marxism, and of mechanically applied formulae which have become strait jackets, this revolution sends a fresh, vital breeze out across the world. And yet—precisely, perhaps, because of its vigorous example —the aborted or defeated guerrilla movements in Argentina, the Dominican Republic, Paraguay, Peru, and Bolivia have shown certain vices of imitation or incapacity to adapt the Cuban phenomenon to the conditions of their own struggle. The presence of bearded guerrilleros in a country of smooth-faced Indians like Bolivia is an example of this, although one must bear in mind that the Bolivian guerrilla troop was not able to operate either in the way or in the place that had been anticipated.

In this framework, it becomes important, I believe, to look closely at the alternatives of the revolutionary process in Guatemala where initial guerrilla failures, far from asphyxiating the movement, catapulted it forward. Although the cases are different, the experiences of Colombia and Venezuela, where guerrilla fronts have been consolidated and the fight continues, call for the same kind of thorough examination. The analysis must be based on the *necessity* of extending the revolution from one end to the other of tormented Latin America, so that the struggle against humiliation and misery should be waged on the scale that is indispensable to waging it; and, at the same time, on the *impossibility* of repeating the Cuban experience as it occurred in Cuba. We now know that the bourgeoisie is not again going to paste "Thank You, Fidel" signs on its windshields, nor will imperialism turn a blind eye to the arms traffic nor place its propaganda media at the service of any Latin American revolution. The Dominican invasion and the series of "gorilla" coups d'état in Honduras, Ecuador, Brazil, Bolivia, and Argentina have taught us that imperialism intends to destroy in the egg any attempt at

change in Latin America—no matter how limited—if it is
capable of arousing popular enthusiasm.

DURING OUR TALKS César Montes put special stress on the
Guatemalan character of the revolutionary movement he
heads, in contrast to the *North American* character of the
purportedly Guatemalan forces which have tried to drown it
in blood. Cuba offers Guatemala the rich experience of Latin
America's first successful socialist revolution and the living
example of her people's bravery: a people who broke the myth
of the impotence of the oppressed and, by the force of simple
faith, multiplied their capacity to resist the enemy's threats
and clouts. But the Guatemalan guerrillas' arms and funds
come from Guatemala itself. The revolutionary movement's
tactics and strategy arise out of the terrain on which it operates,
and are proudly nourished on the sap from its own historical
roots, planted deep in its own soil. These lads are not unaware
of their place in contemporary time and space. They understand their role—that they are *making* their revolution out of
their own native clay and the somber stones of their nation's
history. They are not *imagining* some chemically pure revolutionary process conceived in a wishful image or cut with alien
scissors. This explains the break with the Communists and
Trotskyists of the two guerrilla fronts—a revolt against political strategies and patterns of thought which are foreign to
Guatemalan reality. It is also a key to the interpretation of the
recent organic unification of the guerrilla fronts.

THE GUATEMALAN PEASANTS still feel a combative nostalgia for
the revolution which they knew for a decade, and of which the
imperialist aggression robbed them in 1954. The agrarian reform decreed by Colonel Jacobo Arbenz, who headed the
second phase of that bourgeois-democratic revolutionary
period, was the cause of the conflict with the United Fruit Co.
and of the invasion from the north. The government installed
by the CIA tore from tens of thousands of peasant families the

lands they had just received. This is a basic difference between Guatemala and other countries. In Bolivia, for example, the lands distributed by the Paz Estenssoro agrarian reform [1952–1956] were not touched by the military dictatorship of General Barrientos. In that country, imperialism centers its rapacity on the mineral wealth—tin, oil, gas, zinc, iron—but has no investment nor intention to invest in land. From the standpoint of guerrilla influence on the peasants, the importance of this factor is readily understandable: *it cannot but have contributed to the indifference with which Che Guevara was received by the people for whom he offered his life.* In Guatemala, on the other hand, the guerrilleros operate on soil fertilized by the blood and tears of the imperialist and oligarchical restoration on the great banana, cotton, and coffee plantations.

"In all the peasant areas we have visited," César Montes told me, "we easily explain ourselves by saying that the FAR struggle is merely the prolongation by other means of the 1944 revolution. The CIA won and Guatemala lost because that revolution was led by the national bourgeoisie. Now the peasants and working class know that they must not put more trust in other classes than in themselves, in their own strength. Despite its limitations the 1944–54 revolution is a great source of lessons for us and plays an important role as a historic national example of revolution. It has kept the revolutionary flame burning in Guatemala—a unique feature of our country—because it provides a real and living example of what a revolution is. That's a point of reference that anyone can understand." Another important difference from Bolivia is worth mentioning: In Guatemala the fall of the national bourgeois revolution came when it was at its peak, not from its own internal decay.

The guerrilleros do not think that history began with them, on the day the first rebels chose to install themselves in the heart of the Sierra de las Minas. It was the fallen flags of Arévalo and Arbenz that they raised and unfurled. But this *continuation* of the interrupted anti-imperialist process is not

and could not be a *repetition*. The methods of the struggle
change in the same measure as the deepening of its objectives.
Yesterday a national bourgeois revolution fell, without the
capacity or desire to defend itself. The experience of this defeat produced the armed movement which a socialist-oriented
revolution demands today. At this stage of the historical
process, it is increasingly clear that to fight against imperialism
in Latin America is to fight for socialism.

This national and popular intermeshing of the forces under
arms explains the final reunification of the two guerrilla fronts:
the Rebel Armed Forces led by César Montes and the 13th of
November Revolutionary Movement (MR-13), led by Yon
Sosa. César Montes and his men have broken with the Communist PGT; Yon Sosa and his followers broke their ties with
the Trotskyists of the Fourth International (the Posadist
wing). With adjectival differences out of the way, both guerrilla forces rediscovered the essential community of their
nature and aims, the identity of their basic interpretation of
Guatemalan reality and of their resolve to change it by violent
response to the enemy's violence. Breaking away from the
Communist Party apparatus, the FAR guerrilleros charged
that, in the middle of an all-out hunt for revolutionaries and
while "the PGT contributed the ideas and the FAR the
dead," the "top party clique" had served the government as an
intermediary for setting up trade relations with socialist countries. They divorced themselves irrevocably from the "bureau-
crats" serving the international strategy of the U.S.S.R.—"a
narrow sect of defenders of a Marxism-Leninism which is
alien to our people's daily struggle and problems." The MR-13
guerrilleros, expelling the Trotskyists from their ranks, put an
end to the negative influence of rabid extremists who had
sought to give them orders emanating from obscure foreign
basements.*

---

* Four members of the Fourth International, Trotskyists of the Posadas
sect, were expelled from the MR-13 on May 15, 1966. They were accused of
"disloyalty and surreptitious withdrawal of funds." Judged by a broad tribunal

GUATEMALA is an Indian country which betrays itself by being ashamed of its own condition. Most of its people are Indians, but the mestizo population prefers to deny its high proportion of Maya blood: *so it turns against the Indians, transmuting into contempt its impotence to assume its own identity.* Four and a half centuries of racism infect the national and social conscience of the *ladinos.*

Here, as has been clearly said by the late *comandante* Turcios and the present leaders César Montes and Yon Sosa, the socialist revolution has a great task to accomplish in Guatemala: to bring the Indians back into the history from which they have been violently segregated, redeeming the whole society through redemption of its chief victims.

Implementation of the task has been extremely slow. It is long and hard, with more obstacles than visible hopes in the short term; yet without it the revolutionary process would be bottled up inside a war that mestizo and white society wages within itself. The guerrilleros' awareness of the problem is a

---

of guerrilleros and peasants, they admitted having taken substantial guerrilla funds, but said they did it not for their personal benefit but to aid the "Posadista" Fourth International. The tribunal resolved to break all ties with this Fourth International. The guerrilleros escorted the traitors to the frontier of Mexico, their country of origin, warning that if they returned they would be found with faces turned skyward and their mouths full of ants. Shortly before, Fidel Castro had harshly condemned the Trotskyist influence on Yon Sosa's guerrilla group. Launched at the close of the Tricontinental Conference, his attack was considered unfair by many revolutionaries who took an impartial view of the Guatemalan situation.

The final crisis between the FAR and the PGT broke a few months after my interview with César Montes. On January 10, 1968, the FAR command published a statement from the Sierra de las Minas containing serious charges against the Communist Party leadership and announcing a final break. To some extent this was a break between party rank and file and "old guard" leaders. Many FAR cadres were Party members and the FAR had been represented on the Central Committee. In a long statement some days later César Montes confirmed his agreement with everything in the FAR statement. The statement by Montes is reproduced in its entirety as Appendix II (A) of this book.

In a declaration drawn up in February, 1968, in the Sierra de las Minas, the guerrilleros declared the total and definitive unification of FAR and MR-13 in a single organization that would retain the name of Rebel Armed Forces, and unification of command under Marco Antonio Yon Sosa and César Montes. This document is reproduced as Appendix II (B) of this book.

further sign of their genuinely national character and popular vocation. Time presses. The country is persistently invaded by Peace Corps groups and North American religious missions, trained in fluent use of Indian dialects and the arts of capturing these decisive minds, drugged by fatalism and resignation, for the interests they represent. In the document explaining their break with the Communist Party, the guerrillas emphasize that "the work in the Indian peasant sector amounted to nothing; taking off from the false premise that the Indians are 'reserves of reaction,' the Party's national leaders have dedicated themselves to shuffling papers and politicking in the city, and to working with the artisans and trade unions."

THE BOOK that the reader has in his hands was written during the year 1967. It originates in various articles published in the U.S., France, Italy, Chile, and Uruguay, which have been re-worked and much amplified. Events subsequent to the writing of it have not essentially altered the situation. The fall of the most notorious military leaders of the extreme Right, as the consequence of the spectacular kidnapping of the Archbishop and of the failure of the coup d'état that was being hatched, does not signify more than a change of names: this does not mean that the military Right does not continue to wield the real power in Guatemala. The failure of the new attempts at tax reform which the government tried to carry out appears to us to be very significant, as does the subsequent fall of the Ministers of Economy and the Treasury: the government had tried to levy a five percent tax on business transactions, but the oligarchy refused its assent. Consequently, the salaries of the government workers had to be cut (naturally, without touching the salaries of the military) and the budgets of the Institute of Agrarian Reform, Public Health, Housing and Social Welfare were slashed.

The aim of the book is to break down as best it can the wall of deceptions and omissions which blocks the view of the public in many countries. Guatemala, like all Latin America, is the victim of a conspiracy of silence and lies. The masters of the information media fabricate reality according to their convenience. They conceal and deform facts arbitrarily and efficiently, contracting news to the point of disappearance or inflating it to bursting point.

We have sought, then, to retrieve the reality as it is and make it known. The task seems to us more than ever necessary now that Latin America, smitten by treason and disillusion and defeat, needs to rebuild its own hopes as if it were a bombed city.

EDUARDO GALEANO

Montevideo
April 1968

Fury in the Mountains

> *Our hearts rested in the shade of our spears.—Popol Vuh.**

WE HAVE made a halt, and I have emptied over my face what was left in the water bottle. For hours we have been hiking, hiking, hiking up and down over the vertical sierras, cutting our way with machetes through the damp, dense forests. We are not far from the shore of the big lake; with the first light of dawn, veils of mist spread and break over the thickets like fat waving lianas. I am ashamed because I am cold. Even if the leg muscles tighten up like fists, hiking is better than a vain attempt to sleep on a bed of leaves with no covers and with one's breath freezing on one's body. But there is no sweat left in the bodies of my companions, and for them neither cold nor sleep matters. This shame that spreads over me—a repository of city poisons, without experience of the outdoors—is a preview of what I will feel when we reach the camp that César Montes and his guerrilla nucleus have improvised somewhere in western Guatemala. In the company of this handful of boys who live dying and killing for the revolution, I shall be, as someone or other said, "a serious case of virginity."

Many times we have descended one mountain and ascended another: it isn't easy to locate this patrol, which is on a scouting mission far from the usual zone of operations. The guide, an Indian who is always silent, leaves us for a few moments. He climbs the slope to the top, shut from sight by scrub be-

---

* The *Popol Vuh* is the sacred book of the Maya-Quiché Indians of Guatemala. Based on oral traditions, it is known through a 16th-century version written in Spanish by a converted Quiché.

tween the tall trees, to check on certain signs in the neighboring heights. We light cigarettes, my two guerrilla companions and I. We sit on fallen treetrunks in a small clearing. Someone tells a joke. I inhale the smoke and discover that weariness doesn't close my eyes—perhaps because the night still lingers and the cold, up here, is still stronger than the weariness. The guide returns with good news: only another hour's march. We get on the move again. At a certain altitude the Indian points vaguely to one side of the hill and says: "It's there, around there." Nothing is visible but thick jungle. We continue walking in silence. Now the sky can be seen toward the east. The sky seems to be celebrating something. Something like its own sacrifice: its veins have been opened; it is morning.

THEY CALL César Montes "El Chirís," which is a Guatemalan word for "kid." Small, lean, with fine features, a scarf always protecting his delicate throat, César has absolutely nothing of Fidel Castro's imposing figure. "Don't ask me to look fearsome for your picture," he says, laughing, "because no one will believe it." But he has compensated with revolutionary willpower for what he lacks in physical strength. There is a tough, brave, shrewd man behind the innocent expression of this boyish face.

Shorthand history of a rebel: At thirteen, expulsion from a Catholic school, explosion of fury over the fall of the Arbenz revolutionary government; at eighteen, student demonstrations, unarmed comrades falling and spilling their blood, first imprisonment; at twenty, the die is cast, the challenge accepted, violence chosen, time to take to the sierra—marching until one is ready to faint, with teeth clenched, without complaint or asking for respite. At twenty-five, leader of one of Latin America's most important guerrilla movements. They say that even the snakes respect him, just as they say that Yon Sosa fools the soldiers by sleeping in the belly of an alligator.*

---

* In Guatemala myths are not exclusive to rural areas. In the capital, the Alfa Romeo achieved magical prestige because it was said to be the car used by guerrillas to escape from police patrols.

The previous leader of the Rebel Armed Forces, Luis Augusto Turcios, was also a legendary figure for the peasants, who attributed supernatural virtues to him. He was a hot-blooded young officer who learned the technique of the guerrilla from the Yanquis themselves—in a course at Fort Benning, Columbus, Ga., on how to combat it. Dictator Peralta Azurdia put a price on his head and he put one on dictator Peralta Azurdia's. After he took to the hills in 1960, he mocked at death a thousand times. Absurdly, death won because his car caught fire on the highway.

Before joining the guerrillas, Rocael was a soldier. He has experience in the repression of student demonstrations. César Montes, too, but on the other side—as a student. The soldier and the student met and began sharing the same dangers and hopes, trailed by death and eluding it together. Rocael is thirty-six. "The grandaddy of us all," says César. "You've even got rheumatism, eh, Rocael? All of us FAR leaders are very young. Manzana (Apple), as we call him because he's so pink, came to the mountains when he was seventeen; now he's twenty and leads the guerrillas in the northernmost area of the Sierra de las Minas, near Teculután. Camilo Sánchez, second in command of the Edgar Ibarra front, is twenty-four. So is Lieutenant Androcles Hernández, who is just like Shaw's Androcles."

"Are most of the guerrilleros students?"

"Oh, no. Students play a big role in the city, but not in the mountains. There are only a few of them. Most of the guerrilleros are peasants of the area of operations. Manzana doesn't have one student in his lot."

A man appears with canteens full of water. Some guerrilleros clean their rifles; others talk in low voices. "How long will it take to get there?" asks Rocael. "Around ten hours," says Néstor—Néstor Valle. "Okay, let's divide it this way—eight hours here resting and two hours marching," a third suggests. Everyone laughs. "Pure demagogy," says César. A good companion, the wisecrack: the lads know that this lightheartedness must be preserved, defended as if it were water or salt—something of top importance in the guerrillero's life. When the talk turns to hot political problems, and I answer César's questions about the terms of Soviet financial aid to the Brazilian government, he gets very serious, his hands clasped, his eyes fixed on the ground as he scrapes it with his foot. "But look . . . think how many years the Guatemalan revolution could be advanced with so many millions of dollars. . . ." He strokes the point of his beard. Suddenly this Communist of a new independent generation, fed up with bureaucratic stuffiness, smiles mischievously and says: "These Russians are capable of inventing aspirin and headaches at the same time."

In the most dangerous moments the guerrilleros never lose their sense of humor—which doesn't mean they lose their sense of discipline. They have simply discovered that the two are not incompatible. "Better to die happy, no?" says one to me. Death: the guerrillero knows it is always more possible than victory. In one recent action Arnaldo and his patrol died. Humberto Morales, "the bearded one," sold out his comrades for a few quetzales and promises. He disclosed the exact location of a patrol which had gone down to hit the army, and the patrol was wiped out. Among guerrilleros killed in the first months of 1967 was Otto René Castillo, whose charred body was found in Zacapa. Castillo was considered Guatemala's best young poet. He had been exiled ("exile is a long, long lane where walks sadness") and had returned to his land to fight; prophet of his own fate, he had written:

> My country, let us walk together, you and I;
> I will descend into the abysses where you send me,
> I will drink your bitter cup,
> I will be blind so you may have eyes,
> I will be voiceless so you may sing,
> I have to die so you may live.

The young FAR *jefes* are military and political leaders at the same time. "We are nobody's troops," César Montes says to me. "We don't accept the division between military and polit- ·

ical. Turcios started as a military man and I come from the militant political ranks. Here we all regard ourselves as conscious revolutionaries who use firearms; we try to form our cadres in both senses—to be able not only to defend our ideals and argue for them, but also to make them come true with a gun. Separating the political and the military—in some countries the two practically collide head-on—can only lead to serious mistakes."

THE GUERRILLEROS have camped beside a spring, between high mountains rising vertically on either side as if they had been sliced open.

Rocael looks at the sky. Now that storm clouds darken it, a fire can be lit and water heated for coffee. César Montes takes it with two aspirins which someone digs from the bottom of a haversack. He coughs and curses, angry with himself: this damn throat. . . . More coughing. He has caught himself a fine cold. But one must stay on one's feet. The right to be sick is not the only one that guerrilleros lose in the mountains. Yesterday the men of this patrol ate wild leaves boiled with salt. Tomorrow, who knows? Tonight they must march. Mobility is the guerrillero's best weapon. Resting one's feet for too long can mean death.

César Montes refuses a cigarette with a wave of pained resignation. Losing the taste for tobacco is worse than a fever. Great company in the mountains, the cigarette. The guerrilleros smoke "Payasos" of black tobacco, costing six centavos a pack. We talk beneath an improvised tent made of four poles and some greenish nylon, the kind the army has ordered Guatemalan merchants not to sell. Everyone has eaten his ration of the canned meat we brought from the city. The cans were an additional weight on our backs as we trekked up, but the small effort was well worth it. Eating meat seems like a victory, following the army's discovery of a couple of food caches the men were counting on. It's hard to march without having anything to eat at the weary day's end. This risk has to be taken

like so many others. The guerrilla band is in constant movement. It installs itself in a place which it will soon abandon,
after burying leftover food and scattering the campfire ashes.
"The more uncomfortable the guerrillero is, the more secure,"
as Che Guevara wrote. "Hit and run": descend when the enemy ascends, ascend when he descends.

"Our tactics follow from the situation we're in," César explains. "Numerical disadvantage, not enough weapons, lack of
organization, making our own experience. We FAR leaders
have learned war by making war, not in any military school.
And we've been defeating the army during these years—four
years of struggle it'll soon be—without having taken any military courses.

"We have a very special type of mountain," he tells me.
"The Sierra de las Minas runs parallel to the highway that's
most important for export, along which products move to the
Atlantic ports. So the army can put as many troops as it likes
along the whole length of the highway and of the Sierra, and
send them up the mountains when it chooses. It isn't like other
ranges—for example in Santa Cruz, Bolivia, where the mountains are difficult of access in that part of the Ñancahuazu
gorge, or the Sierra Maestra which is at the tip of Cuba with
the road stopping short of there. Here, paths lead up into the
Sierra from the highway itself, greatly easing the strain on the
army. We used to play the cat-and-mouse game, descending
and ascending so as to keep them always below us. But right
now they completely control the highway and send troops up.
So we have to work out new tactics, correct our methods, advance along new lines."

The military campaign launched on a grand scale to finish
off the rebels has not succeeded. It is of small importance that
the guerrilleros have lost geographic control of certain areas,
when they retain intact the sympathy of the people who live
there. Although it has fallen back from its habitual terrain,
the guerrilla troop keeps its feet. The blow has been warded
off. Mobility is the key. "Our columns move fast," says César.

"For that reason they couldn't wipe us out. We have patrols operating in distant parts of the country. They could never capture our camps, for a simple reason: we never had any. We never had fixed camps. All they found were food dumps which we left behind precisely to make marching easier."

"How many miles a day do you march?"

"To give you an example, the guerrilla has marched from Lake Izabal to San Agustín Acasaguastlán—a long way in any man's language, across the steepest mountains in Guatemala and through a whole area without roads. We made that trip in twenty days, without resting a single day, sleeping on the march and with two meals, breakfast before taking off and supper before dark. We hiked from six A.M. till about four or five P.M. That gave us time to cook by daylight and then sleep.

"We would be crazy," the FAR *comandante* went on, "to sit in our camp when they send troops or to try to take on their much bigger forces—better trained, better equipped, with all their logistical support. Nevertheless they start from the premise that we'll stay put for them. On one occasion we had captured a traitor, a stooge of theirs who was informing on people of his own village, and the guy got away. Well, this man gave them complete information on our whereabouts. We simply moved from where we were to the next mountain, a place in Usumatlán that they call 'El Alto.' That was when the Minister, Arriaga Bosque, made a fool of himself saying he had personally gone to take part in the bombings and had proven their efficacy, as if it was possible to 'prove' something from a plane. The bombing lasted an hour and forty-five minutes, against a camp that was already empty. It was childish to imagine that on the third day we'd still be there waiting for them to come and kill us. We watched the whole show from the next mountain, saw the three types of plane—the C-47 jets, the T-33's, and Mustangs—the helicopters and light aircraft. They burned peasants' crops, machine-gunned a lot of cattle, then landed and ate them."

IN 1960 LUIS AUGUSTO TURCIOS, with other members of the
Child Jesus Fraternity military club, rose against the Ydígoras
government; they failed. The organizational weaknesses of the
rising reflected another, deeper disorientation. Those young
officers did not know very well what they wanted, though they
knew pretty well what they didn't want. Another officer involved in that abortive coup, Yon Sosa, "El Chino," now
commands the MR-13 guerrilla front which controls part of
Izabal in northeast Guatemala. Yon Sosa, like Turcios, had
been trained in the United States. He had studied counterguerrilla techniques at Fort Gulick, Panama Canal Zone.

The guerrillas of Yon Sosa and César Montes are now
reunified after a period of violent disagreement. The re-
conciliation has been helped by certain internal changes in
both camps. Tactical differences in the forms of operation
of the two guerrilla groups are not as strong as the identity of
their objectives. They coincide on what is fundamental. Says
César Montes: "All these Indian *compañeros* whom you see
here in the camp are Catholics, fervent Catholics. The fact
that some Communists are in the FAR doesn't mean that our
movement functions as the fighting arm of any party. The
FAR isn't the fighting arm of the PGT. Ours is a broad patriotic movement with a very simple program: that we ourselves,
as Guatemalans, can lead against any foreign intervention,
military, economic or political. We build the people's organization for revolutionary war; in the guerrillas is the seed of the
great popular army which will eventually be able to offer an
alternative power." *

---

* The OLAS solidarity conference, held in Havana in mid-1967, showed the
FAR's independence once more. The Guatemalan delegation was made up of
FAR and PGT (Communist) militants; members of the MR-13 guerrilla
group, who were to have joined the delegation, could not do so for practical
reasons. When the time came to vote, Guatemala joined the majority in con-
demning the apostate position of the Venezuelan Communist Party, but ab-
stained on the secret resolution against technical and financial aid by the
U.S.S.R. and other socialist countries to oligarchical and dictatorial regimes in
Latin America. In the meeting of the commission considering this problem,
Néstor Valle, a guerrillero whom I had the honor to meet in the mountains,

Both Yon Sosa and César Montes underline the importance of "armed propaganda," although they apply it in different ways. The guerrilleros enter the villages, occupy them for some hours, explain to the peasants the reasons for the struggle they are carrying on, and leave behind them organized cells of clandestine resistance in each community. In the case of MR-13, the guerrilleros create, in addition, "peasant committees" which dispute the *real* authority in each village with the military commissioners and the auxiliary mayors, impart justice "outside the framework of bourgeois justice," coordinate efforts to repair the damage the army provokes in its incursions into the zone, and economically sustain the families of comrades incorporated into the guerrilla struggle or killed by the army. For some time, these committees have left in the hands of the clandestine cells the task of the distribution of propaganda materials. The committees have a public existence, and are appointed in an assembly of all the inhabitants of the village.

The FAR, on the other hand, considers that this method leaves the militants an open and easy target for repression: when the guerrilleros leave, the army kills their representatives. The nuclei of the FAR always operate underground.*

talked against the position of another Guatemalan—a Communist of an earlier generation—who had on his conscience certain duties of PGT loyalty to the U.S.S.R. When these two opposing positions were taken, the Guatemalan delegation's vote was neutralized and had the effect of abstention.

* In the course of our talks, César Montes expressed strong disagreement with what Régis Debray writes about "armed propaganda" in his book *Revolution in the Revolution?* "Undoubtedly," Montes said, "Debray's theses are valuable. He has a thorough knowledge of the Cuban experience. He had access to many documents that were completely unknown. But he doesn't know much about the Guatemalan experience. He only knows some aspects from people who have been in our movement but have lived abroad for some time. On other movements I think he also knows relatively little. It isn't underrating Debray to suggest that he is an adventurer in his expressions, but I think the situation as it exists in each country, and the application that is made in each country of the measures which he criticizes, need deeper analysis. In Cuba the guerrilleros never held 'armed propaganda' meetings. But then they didn't need to." Despite these considerations, Montes feels that Debray's work has played an important role in helping the Latin American revolution to acquire an understanding of itself.

Explaining the importance of "armed propaganda," Yon Sosa says that, from the MR-13 viewpoint, machine-guns, rifles and grenades are not the chief weapons in the mountains; they merely provide a secure base for the contact with the peasants. The chief weapon is the word, and the best defense is support from the people. "The peasants are the guerrillas' eyes and ears," El Chino explains.* "We always know what the enemy is doing, and the enemy never knows what we're doing. He would have to destroy the whole population to lick us. But before that happens, we will have pulverized him."

And César Montes says: " 'Armed propaganda' plays an important role in turning the peasant population toward the revolution. Consider eastern Guatemala today. In spite of ferocious repression, Zacapa and Izabal are the vanguard of the revolution. Don't forget that no rural proletariat exists there, only small landowners and sharecroppers who rent land. Yet right now they are resisting the biggest military offensive. Why? Because of 'armed propaganda.' It was thanks to this that the peasants joined in the struggle. We have men who work with us by night and work the soil by day. By now 'armed propaganda' isn't necessary in the east, because the peasants know who we are and what we want, and anyway the army's offensive rules it out at the moment. We consider it essential, though, for our work in new zones, such as the job we are now planning."

A SHARP CRACK, or a human voice imitating a bird's song. The conversation is often interrupted; long minutes of silence and tension follow, fingers ready on triggers. "Was that a shot?"

---

* I wanted also to visit the Izabal mountains to talk to Yon Sosa. It was not possible. MR-13 militants in the city brought me a note from him explaining why he could not receive me: "We are the first to deplore it," he wrote, "but it can't be helped." The statements quoted here come from a tape to which these militants let me listen. The theses of Yon Sosa were set forth extensively in Adolfo Gilly's reportage in *Monthly Review* (May and June, 1965). However, the Trotskyists' expulsion has changed radically the framework of things described by Gilly; moreover, he wrote his articles before the crisis which caused a temporary rift between FAR and MR-13.

a guerrillero whispers. But it's only a far-off woodsman. "No, a stick breaking." The sentries notice the smallest strange noise; any suspicious sound can be the signal for the patrol to take off again, or for forcing it into some unexpected action— an ambush, a skirmish, a battle. "If a spy appears, let him have it."

Here, in the heart of these craggy mountains, the distant sound of a cypress struck by an axe can be mistaken for a shot; a small animal can shake a thicket just as well as an intruding soldier.

The danger has passed. I walk beside César, glancing at the guerrilleros' weapons: a couple of Thompson machine-guns, caliber .45; some Belgian Brownings and other automatics, Swedish and German; Garand World War II rifles; a few M-1 carbines; the legendary .45 Colts. "The Army says it's always capturing arms from us and killing our guys. But they've never been able to exhibit a single weapon of ours that was Cuban or Czech or Chinese or Soviet, nor the body of a single Cuban soldier from our ranks. That would be impossible because it's we ourselves who are making our revolution, with our own men and our own resources. Our men don't come from Cuba. Nor do our weapons, as the Army says they do. They come from the Army itself—we take them in our operations, fighting, or we buy them. Soldiers as well as officers sell arms. If these military chaps are capable of selling their country, why wouldn't they be capable of selling their weapons?

"We've made public our sources of money. We get it by kidnaping big capitalists who for years have been exploiting the labor of Guatemalan workers. Thus we restore to the people part of the wealth stolen from them. We always pick foreign firms or Guatemalan exploiters whom everybody hates." In Guatemala the guerrilleros, their money, and their arms are as Guatemalan as the economic, social, and political problems which account for their advent and survival.

Good lessons from the graves of Vietnam. North American

"advisers" have decided that the Guatemalan army must now combine terror with demagogy in counter-guerrilla operations. The powdered milk, the health centers, the wheat flour now reach the villages together with the threats, the tortures, and the murders. "It's what they call a 'security belt,'" says César Montes. "They do their job in mechanical fashion. They've read in Mao's books that the guerrilla is to the people as the fish to water; they know that on weekends, when they pull fish out of the water, the fish die. They think they can isolate the guerrillas the same way."

Isolate or eliminate the guerrillas without tearing out their roots, as if they were some mere accident of nature lying on the ground, or some satanic Cuban plot! The fact that the rebel voice of Radio Havana can be tuned in on any radio by an illiterate Guatemalan does not explain the guerrilleros' deep roots in the peasantry. Fundamentally it is the peasants' own long experience of suffering and betrayal. What is now being fired from guns is the protest of a people who have not forgotten that foreign intervention denied their right to govern themselves in those tragic days of 1954.

How can an Alta Verapaz peasant not recognize this in the example of the lads who have risen in arms, when for two days' work he gets the price of a bottle of milk, and a pound of meat costs as much as his wage for three days? These men without land, forced to work for little or nothing a land almost without men, have learned in the course of their own national revolution and the hard ensuing battles that neither misery nor humiliation is inevitable. The peasants in this little patrol of César Montes explain it to me simply. They tell me that this fight isn't for any one person but for all, and that they joined the rebels "to throw those bourgeois and *gringos* the hell out."

César Montes has in his hand the encyclical of Paul VI, *Populorum Progressio*. He reads from it at random: ". . . the peasants become conscious of their undeserved misery . . . the scandal of shocking inequalities. . . ." He winks: "The

Pope is more intelligent than the Guatemalan Right. Read this and you'll see how exactly he nails down the causes of violence," he says.

NIGHT FALLS. Today the quetzal bird which has visited the guerrilleros at this hour for the past two days has missed the appointment. His red breast and gorgeous plumage had glided into the center of the patch of sky left visible above the camp by the mountains. The quetzal is the national symbol of Guatemala. He is said to have lost his voice when the Mayas were defeated by the Spaniards. Others say he never lost his voice but since then has refused to sing. The fact is that when he is caged, he dies.

A Country Within a Country

*Let all rise up, let everyone be called. Let
there not be among us one group, nor two
groups, who remain behind the others.
—Popol Vuh.*

As IF CLAWED by a giant's nails, the mountains show at the
foot of their stone flanks the signs left by the Indians through
centuries and centuries. From the rock comes the lime necessary for their survival. Farther up, on vast slopes, Indians carve
out with primitive tools their tiny depleted fields. Corn spears
sprout, yielding the grain that must be milled on a stone as
they did it a thousand years ago. That is their diet on the
high plateau of western Guatemala. Tortillas of corn flour and
ground lime, perhaps also beans.

One is amazed by the size of the fields. Most of them would
hardly suffice to bury the owner's body. The western high plateau, kingdom of the *minifundio:* here *minifundios* make up
most of the 270,000 farms which, by official census, average
little more than *one hectare** each. This is the area of greatest
Indian population density in Guatemala. More than half of its
people are pure Indians.

The life of this poor country's poorest inhabitants is disinte-
grating, and the survival of some communities around certain
villages certainly does not stop this process. What remains
today of the Mayas who dazzled the scholar Silvanus Morley
into calling them the most splendid indigenous people on the
planet? Four and a half centuries of continuous exploitation
by the conquistador and his sons have not failed to leave their

---

* One hectare equals 2.471 acres.

mark. Crushed by the miserable and humiliating life they have
had to live, the present descendants of the Quichés and other
Mayan tribes have almost lost sight of their past cultural splen-
dors. They form a kind of country within a country, distinct
and distant from the country of men with white skin (of
whom there are indeed few) or the more numerous ones of
mixed blood. (The word *ladino* as used in Guatemala covers
both the mestizo and the white.)

But this Guatemala within Guatemala is a conquered,
broken country. In remote epochs its antecedents created
great architectural works, testaments in stone to their passage
through history. The present Mayas build only their own sor-
did hovels. The ancient Mayas celebrated life, elevated its most
diverse aspects to divine categories. Today the Holy Week pro-
cessions produce sad exhibitions of collective masochism: they
drag heavy crosses, participate in the flagellation of Jesus step
by step on the interminable ascent to Golgotha; with dolorous
wails they convert his death and burial into a cult of their own
death and burial. (The Indians' Holy Week ends without a
resurrection.) When victory is talked about in the language of
the Conquistador's culture, the Indians celebrate their own
defeat. To know this, it is enough to see their dances or listen
to that rancorous silence which replaces the songs they no
longer sing.

The white man's churches supply new symbols and media
of expression to the world of superstition and magic which the
Indian inherited. In the Catholic temples, built on the ruins
of the old pagan ones, he prays or mutters to his conquered
gods. He seems to see their faces wreathed in heavy incense
behind the idols erected in their stead. But he is praying
against the bad luck his best friend will bring him. He will
pay the sorcerer to curse the rival family with God's blessing.
When they are not expressing distrust or hatred, these lips
whisper prayers for money or protection—against the snake,
for example (which scarcely exists in the high plateau), perhaps because it symbolizes the evils of life here below. Only

in the exquisite colors of hand-loomed cloth does the impulse of the original civilization, whose ultimate expressions were crushed by the Conquest, seem to survive. In the crude pottery of today, no trace remains of the skill of the old masters.*

IN THE COURSE of our conversations, the guerrilla *comandante* César Montes tells me: "It's no secret to anyone that our peasant problem will be resolved by the integration of the Indians, through the struggle, into national life." This is the key to the period ahead. The Indians' attitude will be decisive in the Guatemalan revolution. What will be their response to the challenge of the battle that is already being fought in their name and that of all exploited Guatemalans? Will they recognize their own lost voice in the protest that is being expressed with bullets? Some Indians have been fighting with the guerrillas from the very first. César Montes unfolds before me an Esso map: "The Edgar Ibarra guerrilla front was first opened up in the Sierra de las Minas area. As you can see here, the Sierra is to the east. Half of it lies in Zacapa and El Progreso departments with a tip in Izabal. On the other hand, in Alta Verapaz to the north you have a completely Indian area speaking Kekchí. We developed our front in those mountains and speared out toward various places in the plains. The Sierra de las Minas guerrilla is made up of Alta and Baja Verapaz Indians—*Verapaces*, as we call

---

* The hypocrisy of the *ladino* bourgeoisie and middle class has no limits. They worship Tecún Umán, legendary leader of the Mayas, as a national hero, and become emotional about the feats attributed to him, but their deeds show a more racist mentality than that of Pedro de Alvarado, Cortes' ruthless lieutenant. The beautiful native cloth, whose colors and designs perpetuate the best of the unexterminated Maya traditions, can be found only in the homes of a few foreigners of good taste in the capital. For the bourgeois or middle-class Guatemalan, whether white or mestizo, it would be out of the question to decorate his home with the products of an inferior race, something between man and other animals. He prefers horrific reproductions of storm-tossed ships, or no less gruesome dancing girls of plastic or glass, to the magnificent native craft of weaving. The bad conscience of the white or mestizo Guatemalan masks his need for revenge. He transfers to the Indian the contempt he himself receives from the *gringo*. And the *gringo*, the North American, can, as we know, only be scorned by God.

them—and peasants from other areas. We have carried out actions in all these areas including Panzós, the heart of the Alta Verapaz Indian region. . . ."

"What kind?"

"Military actions and armed propaganda meetings."

"How did it go in Panzós, for example?"

"Well, we took it and afterwards held a meeting. A guerrillero of our front, who knew Kekchí, spoke."

"Did you make people come to the meeting?"

"It was done like this: After the battle, the people were very afraid. So we took the municipal building where there was a loudspeaker. We started calling the people and explaining what had happened and why. People started coming near. . . . Many had hidden themselves in the mountains or shut themselves up in their homes, but when they heard the words of revolution in their own language, they got interested and came out."

"What did you promise them? Land?"

"Promise? We promised them nothing. We promised them a struggle; we urged them to fight for their rights, for the things they needed."

"But what demands . . . ?"

"The guerrillero is essentially an agrarian fighter. Our country is pre-eminently agrarian. We seek different solutions for different areas, different problems. The truth is that the *mini-fundio*, like the *latifundio*, has done plenty of damage to Guatemala. Our chief demand is land, under a single slogan which embraces all forms of land tenancy and all possible solutions: *Land to him who works it*, in one form or another."

ONE OF THE GUERRILLAS' biggest losses was the death of Emilio Román López, "Pascual," a Verapaz native, Protestant, who was the FAR's second *Comandante General*.* Pascual had

---

* He was riddled with bullets on October 2, 1966, in the office of a dentist opposite La Parroquia church. Usually he never left the mountains, but an unbearable toothache was his undoing. Pascual put up brave resistance; at the cost of his own life he covered with his gun the escape of other guerrilleros through the ravines.

great influence on the Indian population of his area. He kept
in close touch with Indian peasants who went down to pick
coffee and cotton on the southern slopes and in the Pacific
plain.

Guatemala's economy rests on the aching shoulders of
countless Indian men, women, and children who each year
make the long trek from the *minifundios* of the western high
plateau and the long-suffering lands of Alta Verapaz, down
south to the *latifundios* which hire field hands. Many are sent
down in trucks, like cattle, by those who hire them; others
make the interminable walk. Necessity does not always make
the decisions; sometimes it is liquor. What often happens is
that the hiring agents pay a marimba orchestra and see that
strong alcohol circulates freely. When the Indian recovers
from his spree, he has debts to pay. He will pay them working in hot strange lands, whence he will return after some
months with perhaps a few centavos in his purse, perhaps with
tuberculosis or malaria. The army is around to "convince"
Indians who resist being moved, hauling them forcibly out of
their houses.*

Despite the views of some North American anthropologists,
who have all the vices of electronic computers and none of
their virtues, the Indians *participate* in the country's total

* International organizations estimate that between 150,000 and 200,000
agricultural workers migrate at harvest times with their families to coffee
plantations. When the coffee is harvested they go down to the coast to work
on cotton and sugar plantations. The technician Sergio Maturana writes:
"One is struck by the relatively high percentage of family workers, which
is due to the predominance of very small farms (of the *minifundio* type).
Thus, for example, the number of active workers estimated as available
in mini-farms (less than 0.7 hectares) was 111,500, while the census showed
only 68,900 men over fourteen years of age. The discrepancy could seem to be
accounted for by the seasonal workers on the other types of farms, especially
medium and large ones. Although the same phenomenon could appear in the
'sub-family' (very small) farms, it was not possible even indirectly to determine
its magnitude. It is known that great numbers of high plateau workers go to
labor on the big coastal farms, often accompanied by their wives and children."
The National Indian Institute estimates that some 160,000 persons go down
from the high plateau every year, of whom only two percent definitely remain
on the coast. Above a certain age, Indians will not leave their traditional territory. They don't go to the "hot lands" because they want to die in the "holy
land."

economy. They participate as victims, but they participate.
They buy and sell a good part of the few things they consume
and produce, at the mercy of powerful and greedy dealers who
charge much and pay little. Day-workers on plantations, and
government soldiers in the mountains, they spend their lives
toiling and fighting. Indian society does not exist in a vacuum
outside the general framework. It forms a part of the economic
and social order, its members playing the hard role of the most
exploited among the exploited. The rising Indian bourgeoisie
of Quezaltenango, small and weak, proves by exception the
situation in which the heirs of the Mayas live. The key to
their liberation is the key to the country's liberation: Will
they discover the identity that unites them to the other Guatemalans exploited by the oligarchy and by imperialism? Will
they fight shoulder to shoulder with the other peasants and
workers of Guatemala against their *criollo** and foreign oppressors?

A typical monoculture and export economy, the Guatemalan economy depends on this annual mass shift of seasonal
workers to harvest the coffee and cotton for starvation wages.
Capitalism, it is said, creates the means of its own destruction.
Down there on the coast the Indians come in contact with
a new, different reality, forced by circumstances to share the
fate of other wage workers—mestizos or, very exceptionally,
whites. Although most of the Indians can't speak Spanish,
reality thus begins to speak to them in a language of deeds,
not words, of the exploitation they suffer in common with
their class brothers.

I ASK CÉSAR MONTES to what extent or in what way the FAR
makes contact with the Indians, once they have been removed
from their "natural" mode of existence. "The struggle can
develop in various ways," he says, "and not only through a
guerrilla front as we did it in Zacapa. Those Indians met people
of ours who opened their eyes to a series of struggles that

---

* *Criollo:* person of Spanish descent born in Latin America.

the peasants in the south of San Marcos, and in Suchitepéquez, Retalhuleu, Escuintla, and Santa Rosa, are able to carry on. When the Indians get involved in the economic life of those places, they realize that it's possible to win new gains. They wait half a year for harvest time, vegetating in their high plateau areas. When they go down to the south coast, disillusion awaits them. One wage scale is offered and another is paid. They are offered a certain period of work and it turns out to be less. The conditions are subhuman. The government cracks down on any attempt to organize peasants. Everything is so backward in this country that any labor organization to defend purely economic rights is 'communist.' Even unions organized by the Christian Democrats are attacked—and in Guatemala, Christian Democracy is more reactionary than anywhere in Latin America. Yet they are attacked. Not only that: there was the case of a peasant in El Progreso, a Christian Democrat, who was a trade unionist and spent more than eighteen months in jail, accused of being a guerrillero.

"Here trade unionism is synonymous with communism. And that's the problem all over the south coast. The peasant organizations of Suchitepéquez and Retalhuleu—peasant leagues as they're called—have been relentlessly hounded and their leaders jailed. As part of the new government's propaganda campaign, they took eight peasants from their homes in La Máquina, in Suchitepéquez Department, murdered them, and left the bodies lying in the middle of the jail. They had nothing whatever to do with us. Yet the press afterward reported that they'd tried to ambush an army patrol and were a south coast group of guerrilleros."

"As the counterrevolution advances, the revolution develops," César Montes often says during our talks. In fact the military "surround and kill" campaign, and the terror let loose by the army through its "White Guards," have resulted in the guerrilla band's tactical withdrawal from its old stamping grounds and extension into new areas. It tries out new methods and learns more about the characteristics of each zone, each sector of the population. In the purely Indian areas it has to do "a patient job, a careful job." Describing some of the difficulties, Montes speaks of North American intervention disguised under the Peace Corps and of the various religious missions "which for a long time have been deforming the Indian's mentality so as to keep him out of the political struggle, the struggle for genuine economic solutions. They concentrate on his talents as an artisan although obviously the peasant problem in this country, still less the Indian problem, won't be solved by weaving and pottery."

A personal experience in connection with the Peace Corps' economic solutions comes to my mind as we talk. Some friends and I had disembarked at the Indian village of Santiago de Atitlán after crossing the magnificent lake. The children surrounded us crying "Teikapichi, Teikapichi!" Being new in Guatemala I thought this must be some phrase in the local dialect. I was quickly set straight. It turned out to be their version of "Take a picture!" which they had learned to say to get a tip from camera-buff tourists.

Neither primitive farming in the unproductive *minifundio*, nor tourism, nor folk crafts, can bring the Indian into civilization with the rights that modern life concedes to a human being. The Indian is integrated into the society of "the others" to the extent that it *uses* him. The picking of coffee and cotton binds him to the other exploited people. However deep his roots in his own soil, he cannot choose between working for wages and farming for himself. The choice is made in advance: the society which rejects him assigns him the role that makes him acceptable. "There is a close relation between the land shortage and the low farm wage," as the perceptive Guatemalan anthropologist Joaquín Noval notes. Noval has shown that the scarcity of land, added to the poverty and low productivity of the soil, forces the *minifundio* peasant to hire himself out cheaply to the *latifundio* farmer who, to bring this about, fixes rents very high on his vast but minimally exploited properties.

THE GUATEMALAN revolutionary faces great difficulties. High walls separate the Indian from the history that awaits him. Added to the most obvious problem of communication—for he speaks either no Spanish or very little—are other alienations, much more important ones, the fruit of ancient hatreds brewing within him during four and a half centuries of humiliation and treachery. The experience of the Alta Verapaz guerrilleros is eloquent: the revolutionary word has to be spoken by and to the Indian in his own language or it will not be understood.

There are also barriers of distrust confronting any proposal for change. From the Maya religions there survives a static conception of the world which easily fits into the Christian cults. There is a "natural" order of things, as immutable as it is deserved by both victims and victimizers, and a no less "natural" structure of hierarchies determining who gives orders and who obeys them. The Christian churches have exploited the Indians' resignation, fear, insecurity, and lack of confidence, fixing in their minds the idea of sin and punishment, of eternal damnation. When Arbenz tried to bring the Indians into a national mobilization for agrarian reform, he found that the enemy's propaganda campaign had borne fruit: agrarian reform was a dark design of the devil, or a direct threat to the right of property. The Indians were afraid that their one-hectare plots would be expropriated! *

The other important source of culture affecting the Guatemalan Indian is the army. Hunted like wild animals as they leave their fiestas (each army agent must fill his "quota"), young Indians are forced to leave their lands to do military service. Only poor peasants do this service in Guatemala; urban young men easily arrange to avoid it. Some of these poor peasants who go off to be soldiers will never return. When

---

* Nevertheless the revolution was able to improve the Indian's lot. In a short time it did more for him than anything else in Guatemalan history. Among those recognizing the favorable changes were such North American anthropologists and sociologists as John Gillin, Raymond Scheele, Wagley, Robert Ewald, and Morris Siegel.

they die in battle against the guerrilleros, the news is withheld from their families; in some cases they are informed that the soldier "has been sent to Panama with a special scholarship." A friend commented to me: "Here, Panama is another name for winter" (death).

The army merely confirms, by the force of discipline, the fatalistic concept of the world and sacramental respect for the established order of hierarchies. The Indian takes up arms against those who die for him. But at the same time his objective situation makes him especially sensitive to the propaganda of the revolution. Many a soldier has deserted to the ranks of the opponents. For, quotes César Montes, "You can fool some of the people all of the time, or all of the people some of the time, but not all of the people all of the time." He adds, "The peasants need land and don't have it. They need houses but the government builds them for the military. It's an anger bottled up through centuries that is going to explode in Guatemala, that is now exploding."

Brief History of the Victims
and the Rebels

They did not then have fire and Tohil made it and gave it to them, and the people warmed themselves with it, feeling very content with the heat it gave them. The fire was lit and burning when a big rain and hailstorm came and put it out.—Popol Vuh.

"MY PILOTS are blond with blue eyes," Guatemalan ex-President Miguel Ydígoras Fuentes once said, "but that doesn't mean they're North American." In this country of Indians the physical coincidence was hardly accidental. The United States has been intervening in Guatemala's internal affairs for a long time, on every level. The imperial presence in the country is the very essence of crudity—an unadorned model of the exploitation endured by the tormented lands south of the Rio Grande. Guatemala is the clumsily masked face of all Latin America, the face of the suffering and of the hope of our countries, plundered of their wealth and of the right to choose their destiny.

It is from the United States that presidents and dictators are installed and removed in Guatemala. The economy is controlled from Wall Street through investments, trade, and credits. The army receives weapons, training, and orientation from North American officials who often participate personally in military operations within the country. Press and television depend in large degree on the advertising of foreign firms. Officials and technicians of the United States Embassy or "international" organizations operate a parallel government which becomes the only government at decisive mo-

ments. Coca-Cola has replaced natural fruit juices and the God
of the Protestants and the Mormons competes with the Mayan
divinities, who have survived hidden behind Catholic altars.
Of course the domination and exploitation of Guatemala,
as if it were a piece of private property, is nothing new. It has
assumed peculiar characteristics since 1954, because the crimi-
nal invasion which imperialism organized in that year has
marked the country's present history with fire. The fall of
Arbenz was a decisive link in a long chain of aggressions which
neither began nor ended at that point. The present situation
cannot be explained without keeping very much in mind the
revolutionary process of the decade beginning in 1944, and its
tragic end. From those winds come today's storms. The same
forces which bombed Guatemala City, Puerto Barrios, and
Puerto San José at 4 p.m. on June 18, 1954, are now in power.
They exercise *real* power behind the screen of a civilian regime
which hypocritically proclaims itself heir to the defeated revolution. Ever since that disaster the defeated people have been
learning to rise up in other ways. The lost revolution is also
the key to the consolidation and development of today's
guerrillas.

THE COLONY wanted to make itself a nation: until 1944, the
country had been witness and victim of its history but not a
protagonist. For a long time Guatemala's fate had been at the
mercy of foreign money staked by gamblers in Wall Street or
Washington or the Pentagon. Led by university men and
young nationalist army officers, the revolution exploded and
put an end to the long dictatorship of Ubico—an old general
whose pro-German sympathies did not prevent him from serving the interests of North American enterprises, and whose
proclaimed cult of honesty raised no obstacles to his excellent
relations with the local oligarchy.

  This small country of illiterate Indians dying of hunger
raised itself up on two legs. Arévalo and Arbenz, successively
elected by popular vote, had the job of leading the difficult

venture of national affirmation—"national" in a sense that transcended the frontiers of Guatemala. Under these administrations the best and sturdiest efforts were made to rebuild Central America's lost unity on new foundations.

Central America—like all Latin America—was divided up by frontiers which imperialism consolidated or invented, the better to dominate it; and it will not be imperialism that will reconstitute the great fractured motherland. There is as wide a gap between Arévalo's original projects and the present SIECA (Central American Economic Integration) as between the Latin American Free Trade Association (ALALC) and the dreams of Artigas* or Bolívar. So-called "Central American integration," as now being carried out, produces nothing but *disintegration* of the area's weak national industries for the benefit of *integration* of foreign companies. Operations are planned on a regional scale. With markets widened and tariffs and controls eliminated, imperialist plunder takes new and more effective forms. When the Guatemalan revolution tried twenty years ago to bring Central America together economically and politically, the aim was to de-Balkanize the region for the benefit of the region itself; to reply with one voice to the common challenge of underdevelopment, and in ending the fragmentation to make it possible for the poverty and backwardness to be ended. But the Organization of Central American States (ODECA), born of those ideas in 1951, ended up as an enemy of the government of Guatemala. Far from breaking the isolation of the popular revolution, it intensified it. The United States used it as one of the catapults to attack the Arbenz regime, and to demolish it after a long and terrible campaign. Thus SIECA today is a worthy heir to ODECA.

Offshoots of the Guatemalan revolution throughout Central

---

* José Gervasio Artigas (1774–1850), *gaucho* rebel against Spain and Portugal, who led the fight to make of the whole Rio Plata basin (the old viceroyalty of the Rio Plata) one independent nation. However, as a result of the "divide and rule" intrigues of the British Empire he was defeated and the area was broken up into different countries.—*Translator*.

America could have materialized only through other revolutions which never occurred. Guatemala felt nothing but hostility or indifference from its small neighbor countries, ruled by straw men for United Fruit or by life dictators. Yet within the country's borders, the revolution followed its course until its final destruction by troops prepared by the CIA in Honduras and Nicaragua. Its successes are still very much alive in the people's memory. A vigorous educational program was launched; workers of country and city organized into unions protected by the Labor Code. The United Fruit Company, a state within a state, master of the land and railroad and port, exempt from taxes and free from controls, ceased to be omnipotent on its vast properties. The new labor and social security laws enabled the internal market to develop by raising purchasing power and the workers' living standards. Construction of highways and creation of the port at Matías de Gálvez on the Atlantic broke the United Fruit monopoly of transport and trade. Ambitious economic development projects such as electrification of the country were undertaken *with national capital*. As Arévalo said, "In Guatemala we have received no loans, because we know very well that when one gets dollars with the right hand one yields sovereignty with the left." (But this was a very different Arévalo from the man who ended up advising armed intervention against the Cuban revolution.)

Guatemala was beginning to show all of Latin America that a country can break underdevelopment, emerge from misery, without humiliating itself as a beggar at the door of the imperium. There was a new Constitution which for the first time was not a rhetorical trap framed by intellectuals behind the people's backs. Above all there was a new conscience: the obstacles convinced Guatemala of its newborn strength. The Mayas' descendants recaptured a sense of dignity badly wounded by the Spanish conquest and never healed.

On June 17, 1952, the Arbenz government approved the agrarian reform law. In his farewell speech on leaving the government, Arévalo had revealed that his administration had

had to deal with 32 coups d'état promoted by the United Fruit Company. The agrarian reform was "too much": an impermissibly dangerous example for Latin America. The North American Embassy decided that the Arbenz government smelled strongly of "Communism" and was a peril to hemispheric security.* It was not the first time that a bourgeois nationalist regime aiming at independence had been thus described. Certainly neither Arévalo nor Arbenz proposed to socialize the means of production and exchange. The agrarian reform law laid down as its basic objective *the development of the peasant capitalist economy and the capitalist agricultural economy in general.* The other measures taken by both governments were oriented toward the same end. This "confusion" would not be the last, as witness the blood spilled in other countries in years to come. The good health of North American investments south of the Rio Grande and the United States' power politics in its "natural sphere of influence" rest on sacred socio-economic structures which determine that every minute of every day more than one Latin American child shall die of disease or hunger. Whoever touches these structures commits sacrilege: a scandal erupts.

AN OVERPOWERING international propaganda campaign was launched against Guatemala. *That is the plague-spot,* it was proclaimed. "The Iron Curtain is falling over Guatemala." In the first months of 1954 over 100,000 families had benefited from agrarian reform, which *affected only idle lands* for

---

* In 1949 the United States had raised the agrarian reform problem before the United Nations as "a world problem needing urgent attention," and in 1951 a U.N. investigation had noted that Guatemala was one of the countries most needing it. However, in May of 1954, shortly before its fall, the Arbenz government could protest that "the State Department, in the name of the Compañía Agrícola de Guatemala—which, as that official body has stated, is the property of the United Fruit Co.—has brought against the Guatemalan government a formal diplomatic demand for 15,854,849 quetzales with respect to that company's uncultivated lands. These lands were expropriated under the Agrarian Reform law, and the company was paid 609,572 quetzales in accordance with its own tax declarations. The demand—rejected by the government of Guatemala—constitutes open intervention."

which indemnities in bonds were paid to expropriated owners. United Fruit cultivated only eight percent of its properties extending from ocean to ocean; now its vast unused lands began to be distributed among poor peasants who were ready to work them. The president of United Fruit said in a confidential interview: "From here on out it's not a matter of the people of Guatemala against the United Fruit Company: the question is going to be Communism against the right of property, the life and security of the western hemisphere." * The Organization of American States met to give its blessing to the invasion that the CIA was preparing against Guatemala. Among the indignant democrats who then raised their hands to condemn the Arbenz regime at the Caracas Conference were representatives of the bloodiest dictators in the continent's history, living guarantees of Latin American "stability": Batista, Somoza, Trujillo, Pérez Jiménez, Rojas Pinilla, Odría; even now such a conglomeration of corruption would break any computer into which it was fed. "We had neither doubts nor hopes," Guatemalan foreign minister Toriello wrote later about the Conference. That was Guatemala's last chance, on the eve of the agony, to raise its voice for the independent foreign policy which was born of the revolution and died with it. In Chapultepec, San Francisco, Rio de Janeiro, Bogotá, and many other European and American cities, that small voice had spoken loudly and bravely enough to demonstrate, for the United States, inadmissible insolence.

The OAS gave its approval and Castillo Armas—the man-of-the-hour on a white horse, trained at Fort Leavenworth, Kansas—led his U.S.-trained and paid troops into Guatemala. Supported by North American "volunteers" piloting B-47 bombers, the invasion succeeded. Cornered by the enemy, betrayed by his military commanders whom he trusted to the end, Arbenz did not want—perhaps was unable—to fight. On that tragic night in 1954 the people listened on the radio to his

---

* Cited by Guillermo Toriello, foreign minister under Arbenz, in his book, *La Batalla de Guatemala*.

recorded speech of resignation, not to the hoped-for proclamation of resistance.* The same thing was to happen later with leaders of similar movements elsewhere in Latin America. Popular leaders or Presidents with bourgeois-nationalist-type reformist intentions would wind up their days in power by abandoning it without firing a shot. Perhaps scared by the contradictions they had stirred up, and fearing that they would be swamped by the popular forces they had set in motion, neither Perón nor Bosch nor Goulart gave arms to the workers to defend their regimes against the challenge of successive military coups.

Soon after the invasion of Guatemala, Washington officially conceded that the machinery for the crime had been assembled, oiled, and set rolling by North American hands. It was a nice job by the CIA. A year later one of its heads, Gen. Walter Bedell Smith, joined the board of United Fruit, one of whose chairs had already been occupied by the then No. 1 man of the CIA, Allen Dulles. Allen's brother, John Foster Dulles, had been the most impatient of the foreign ministers at the OAS meeting. This is no enigma: it was in his law office

---

* The Argentine journalist Gregorio Selser quotes a dispatch sent at the time by a Venezuelan newsman to his paper, *Ultimas Noticias:* "We, the newspapermen, called the bombers pirate aircraft. They carried no insignia nor flags. As the silvery planes came in sowing death with eight machine guns, women and men fled. The hotel proprietors in Guatemala City made a fortune. There were some three hundred foreign newsmen. I found one of them, my friend Henry Wallace, looking worried: 'I'm getting out,' he said. 'These are Americans and they can be pretty nasty. I'm going to tell them in Havana to send another man.'"

The aerial bombardments went much further than Castillo Armas' troops, who had still only reached Gualán when Arbenz resigned. Guillermo Toriello describes what followed in his book: The North American ambassador, Peurifoy, visited Colonel Carlos Enrique Díaz, who had occupied the presidency and had just dissolved the Guatemalan Labor Party (Communist). The ambassador appeared with a long list of names of revolutionaries in his hand. He demanded that they be shot within twenty-four hours. "But why?" asked Díaz. "Because they are Communists," replied the ambassador. Díaz refused. "The worse for you," warned Peurifoy as he left the room—and Col. Díaz was immediately overthrown by Col. Monzón. Monzón met with Castillo Armas in San Salvador. There an agreement was signed, imposed by Peurifoy with a .45 pistol under his jacket. Afterward the "Yanquimalan" Castillo Armas made his triumphal entry into Guatemala City.

that the contracts between United Fruit and the Guatemalan Government had been drafted in 1930 and 1936.

CASTILLO ARMAS fulfilled his mission. He returned the expropriated idle lands to United Fruit and other landlords, and delivered to the international oil cartel the subsoil of 4,600,000 hectares—almost half of the country. The Oil Agreement was drawn up in English and arrived in English at the Congress. It was translated into Spanish at the request of a deputy who still retained a shred of shame. The revolution had declined to surrender the oil despite the pressures brought to bear during its decade of government. "For whom are you keeping this oil?" "For Guatemala," Arévalo had replied to a Standard Oil agent. Today the cartel keeps in reserve, without exploiting them, the deposits where oil has been located —a policy it also follows in other Latin American countries.

Castillo Armas governed by terror. He closed down the opposition press, which had functioned freely in Arbenz's time, and sent militant democratic politicians and labor and student leaders to jail, to the grave, or to exile. Finally he himself was assassinated. Eisenhower bewailed his death: "It is a great loss for his own nation and for the whole free world," he said. After new elections, which were annulled, and a brief military junta government, Gen. Ydígoras Fuentes became President. Before the Castillo Armas invasion the CIA had invited Ydígoras to head the expedition. He himself now tells how he turned down the offer. Interviewed by the newspaperwoman Georgie Anne Geyer in San Salvador, Ydígoras said that he had hardly won the elections before four CIA men approached him to threaten reprisals if he didn't pay the balance on the $3 million debt incurred by Castillo Armas to finance his glorious invasion.*

---

* Says Ydígoras: "I told them I owed them nothing, that Castillo Armas was dead and that I, far from being his heir, had defeated his movement at the polls. They threatened me with a 'conspiracy of silence' and said that in that case I would get no aid from the United States, and nothing good would ever be written about my government in that country."

Ydígoras put his signature to an unconstitutional and infamous agreement guaranteeing present or future foreign investments, which later served as a model for other Latin American governments with equally dubious ideas about national dignity. He also made his own effort at agrarian reform—a reform with such peculiar characteristics that only big landlords benefited, as a recent official report shows. It was Ydígoras who offered Guatemalan land to train the forces that stormed Cuban beaches in April 1961, in exchange for some commitments to help his government. But in spite of this, his business relations with the CIA continued to be disastrous. He still bitterly complains that the United States did not keep its part of the bargain, and says he obtained the promised sugar quota only after threatening to boycott Alliance for Progress conferences.

ACCORDING TO the *Miami Herald*, which is no more Communist than Lyndon Johnson, the decision to unseat Ydígoras was adopted at a meeting between Kennedy and his "top advisers" early in 1963. The present head of CIA, Richard Helms, was there and so was the then ambassador to Guatemala, John O. Bell. Both showed great concern about a possible new electoral victory for Juan José Arévalo, who had announced his candidacy from exile. They attached no value to Arévalo's repeated blasts against the regime in Cuba, his public denunciations of Castro as "a danger to the continent, a menace." Bell was convinced that Arévalo was "a Communist." His view prevailed despite President Kennedy's doubts. Colonel Peralta Azurdia brought off the coup d'état at the end of March, 1963. Three days earlier Arévalo had secretly entered Guatemala; a journalist interviewed him. This "provocation" was enough to make the military unsheathe their swords.

So began another brutal dictatorship. One of its first acts was the murder of eight political and trade union leaders in

Puerto Barrios, the United Fruit port. Trucks laden with
rocks drove over them, crushing them alive.

Three years later Julio César Méndez Montenegro, a liberal Catholic lawyer who had been involved in the revolution
of ·1944, defeated his two opponents—both colonels—in the
elections. The results were only made public a week after
polling day. By then the winning candidate had been forced
to sign a pact with the purportedly defeated dictatorship.
Among other things the pact provided that the military
commands must remain unchanged; that no officer involved
on the side of the 1944 revolution could fill a post of command in the armed forces; and that Col. Rafael Arriaga
Bosque must remain as Minister of Defense.* Arriaga Bosque
had actively plotted against Arévalo and Arbenz, and later also
against Ydígoras; he had been the "strong man" of the
Peralta Azurdia administration. He was the "strong man" of
the Méndez Montenegro administration (of which Méndez
Montenegro was the "weak man") until his attempted coup
met with failure and the U.S. gave the go-ahead for his replace-
ment. The names changed but the power structure remained
the same. The President plays a pathetic role. He provides
the cover of an apparently civil administration for the military
dictatorship which actually rules. Had it not been for the
above-mentioned pact, the military men would not have
surrendered the government to Méndez Montenegro. Government, not power: Méndez Montenegro's hands are tied. He
survives, openly backed by the United States Embassy, but
only on the basis that he can do nothing. Nothing except
talk with intimate friends in strictly private gatherings about

---

* The Vice President, Marroquín Rojas, has publicly admitted the existence
of this pact. Under it the army "gave" the government party (Partido Revolu-
cionario) a year in which to exterminate the guerrillas. The pact also gave the
army power of veto. The army, for example, vetoed the candidacy of the writer
Mario Monteforte Toledo for the ambassadorship to Mexico, and that of
Colonel Carlos H. Aldana Sandoval, former Communications Minister in the
Arbenz government, who had been nominated to head the FIDEP, an organization for development of the Petén area. Symptomatically, the 22 gov-
ernors named by the Executive for Guatemala's 22 departments *are all colonels.*

his good reformist intentions, receive imposing loans from foreign banks that are mortgaging the country, and watch with impotent complicity the savage violence from the Right. Many activists of the President's own party have been murdered by armed bands which the army organizes and protects: the hunt for Communists and "Communists" has been launched with blind fury in Guatemala.

The Footprints of Terror

> *The bird Xecotcovach came and pecked*
> *out their eyes, another called Camalotz*
> *cut off their hair, the animal called Cotz-*
> *balam devoured their flesh, and the one*
> *named Tucumbalam broke their bones*
> *and tendons.—Popol Vuh.*

IN APRIL 1967, *Time* magazine tells its millions of readers that the situation in Guatemala has "remained quiet" in the recent period. A little before *Time* published this article Julio César Méndez Montenegro, President of Guatemala, summoned a close friend of student-struggle days and said to him: "Don't move from here. Stay and live in the palace. I have learned that you are on one of the 'lists.' They're going to kill you. This is the only protection I can offer." Shortly afterward the chief of one of the extreme right-wing terrorist organizations which are turning the country into a shambles made a sage statement to a Guatemala City daily: "We are concerned to maintain constitutional order. . . . A *de facto* situation would give the guerrilleros a flag to fight for."

Behind the thin screen of the Méndez Montenegro civil regime, the military dictatorship set up by foreign intervention in 1954 is continuing with more violence than ever. Linked to the army by an umbilical cord, the terrorist bands act with complete impunity. The army is master of the situation, and the "constitutional" President washes his hands of it. The terror emerges from the shadows, strikes and fades again into the darkness. A woman's eyes reddened from weeping, an empty chair, a splintered door, someone who won't come back: the crime will simply have been a blow of fate, and the government will join the family in mourning the victims. *Time* forgot to explain in its article *for whom* the situation is quiet. Not for the Guatemalans, certainly. Exploding bombs shake the city at night, terrorists machine-gun people and houses in full light of day, more than five hundred have been threatened with death. The papers supply their readers with a daily quota of corpses which turn up mutilated or burned in the Motagua river, or are found at daybreak in the mountains or beside a road or on the outskirts of a town. Most of these featureless faces will never be identified. The bodies and heads are always mutilated by torture, hands tied behind backs; sometimes some information happens to permit the corpse to be given a name. This decapitated woman in Santa Rosa is the teacher Oaxaca de Mejía, that castrated man is one of the Pineda Longo brothers, that body burned alive is Nora Paíz, that Salamá peasant with pins stuck in his eyes. . . . Many deaths are never even heard about: the victims are poor Indians, without known name or origin, whom the army will include in its reports of victories against the guerrillas. Guatemala seethes with violence. This violence is of the Right. Blind, bloody, indiscriminate repression, in cities and villages, is part of the military "encircle and annihilate" campaign against the guerrillas. Under the legal code now in force, members of the security forces have no judicial responsibility for homicides, and the police version is considered full proof in the courts. Owners and administrators of big estates have the legal standing of local authorities, with the right to carry arms and form repressive forces; the Vice President, Clemente Marroquín Rojas, justifies this because the landlords "constitute the vital source of production." *Time* really meant to say that the situation is "quiet" for these medieval-minded lords of the land, for the five-hundred-odd Guatemalan colonels who respond to the Pentagon like the echo to a voice, and for the Wall Street coupon clippers who multiply their capital invested in Guatemala as Christ multiplied the loaves and fishes.

In a recent pastoral letter the Archbishop of Guatemala spoke of the "peace of the cemetery" which "certain interests" wanted to establish in the country.

After mentioning the havoc caused by systematic terror, the Archbishop thus enumerated the problems of Guatemala:

> No one can deny that our social and economic reality is tremendously unjust and unbalanced; that there has to be a change in our corrupted structures; that above all a transformation of the mentality of many of our fellow-citizens is necessary. The need for a change, and a radical one, is felt in every corner of the motherland. The present unjust distribution of national income, the disparity of earnings—for while a few receive amounts that we do not hesitate to call offensive to the poverty of Guatemala, the immense majority get starvation wages—the fact that only a little more than two percent of the active population owns seventy percent of the cultivable land, creating the grave situation of the *latifundio* in some areas and the even graver one of the *minifundio* in the high plateau; the systems by which our peasants are hired, and which still have no legal standing; the fact that some hundreds of thousands of school-age children are deprived of elementary education; the specter of illiteracy, the disintegration of the family, with its most serious consequences; growing immorality on all sides; and finally the lack of proper education in responsibility and order, not to mention other evils that afflict us, demand the courage to make a thorough change.

It is precisely the gendarmes of this "tremendously unjust and unbalanced social and economic reality" whom the Archbishop was denouncing, those who want to enforce this "quiet" spattered with blood. They are aiming at the "peace" of the cemetery, a typical case of the *pax americana*.

OFFICIALLY, 1967 was designated "the year of peace" in Guatemala. But in the Gualán area no one fishes any more. Too many corpses have been caught in the weirs—*tapexcos*, as they are called—which the fishermen improvise to catch fish. (In

Gualán a group of North American officers are constant
callers at the home of Mariano Sánchez, the army's representative and boss of the local terror.)

The frenzy of the hunt recalls—of course on a smaller scale
—the recent massacre in Indonesia. Under none of Guatemala's former military regimes did terror so seize hold of the
country as under Julio César Méndez Montenegro's civil administration. The armed bands of the extreme Right operate
with impunity and efficiency, protected by the army and police
whose offspring they are. The police wear bullet-proof vests
on the streets, jeeps patrol the capital night and day. The
armed enforcers of the law know their enemies. They grab a
young man, Héctor Berger Mijangos, as he leaves a party one
Sunday night. The youth doesn't understand. He has taken
one drink too many; but he never mixed in politics. He will be
interrogated and beaten for the next three days. Finally, on
Thursday, he will be formally charged with distributing New
Anticommunist Organization [NOA] propaganda on Wednes-
day night—that is, while he was a prisoner in the Fourth Corps
police headquarters. The leaflets he was alleged to have distributed will be shown to the judge. Berger Mijangos will
finally be freed because his lawyer has witnesses who saw him
arrested. But this young man who was ready to live without
commitment to anything will be scared. He will feel under
suspicion and still won't understand. Perhaps he will flee to
Honduras.*

The Telecommunications Authority announces in the press
that "telephones from which anonymous calls are made will be
disconnected." Citizens are warned: "Don't touch suspicious
packages." Threats made directly or by letter or phone are fol-

_____

* Each time that extreme Right activists or military conspirators are arrested, the government feels obliged also to imprison people who have left-
wing ideas or are merely known for their democratic convictions. In November
1966, when it cracked one of the military plots that incessantly threaten it,
the government jailed for a month a number of men who had nothing to do
with the coup d'état conspiracy but whom the security authorities had listed
as Communists. People whose names began with "B" were chosen at random
—Blanco, Bocaletti, Barreda, Barrios, Barrientos. . . .

lowed by kidnapings, murderous attacks, tortures, assassinations. "See a Communist, kill a Communist" is the slogan of the New Anticommunist Organization, whose definition of communism would make the John Birch Society blush for shame. NOA depends directly on the army. It was not poetic license when one of NOA's press releases said that it operates "side by side with the glorious Guatemalan army." It has promised to tear out the tongue and cut off the left hand of its enemies.

As for MANO (the Organized Nationalist Anticommunist Movement) it operates in the orbit of the police.* Six bombs exploded at about 8 P.M. on May 16, leaving a trail of blood; at the same time MANO distributed leaflets in residential areas suggesting that the doors of left-wingers be marked with black crosses. At the bottom of the leaflets were the words: "Guatemala, 1967, month of flowers." Both NOA and MANO have published confidential data which were in the possession only of the army or the political police. Luis del Valle was found dead, a victim of frightful tortures, three days after police arrested him at the end of June 1967. MANO announced that it had killed him and tossed the body onto the highway.

"Your days are numbered; MANO isn't playing games," say the personal warnings. CADEG, the Anticommunist Council of Guatemala, announces that it will cleanse the country of Communists in a week. The terrorist groups customarily operate through "military agents" designated by the army, who are the *real* power in Guatemala's interior. The authority of auxiliary mayors, elected by the civil power, is purely nominal. Thus the tragedy of the whole country is reproduced in every

---

* MANO first announced its existence on June 3, 1966, a month before Méndez Montenegro assumed the presidency. A white hand appeared over a red circle framed in black, with these words below: "This is the hand that will eradicate national renegades and traitors to their country." When it began operations, the president announced that he would apply "the inexorable weight of law and justice" against terrorist organizations.

little village. Violence defines positions: the boss is the one who commands, not the one who says he commands.

But the armed bands also have other elements at their disposal. It is not hard to extend the hours of a soldier or have him change into civil garb for an "extra" job. The professional army believes its very survival is at stake; it is ready to toss a coin, winner take all, for its right to live—for its giant slice of the budget. As in Vietnam, it is easy enough to claim "self-defense."

A revolver is put in the hand of a rural landowner, perhaps possessing only medium or small holdings but haunted by the nightmare of a possible social revolution which he thinks will destroy his order of values and material and moral security: a murderer is created by a few words breathed in his ear. Sometimes, too, terrorists are recruited at random. Oliverio Castañeda lived in a village in Teculután, in Zacapa, off the map between river and mountain. "You helped the guerrillas; we're going to kill you and your family," the soldiers told him one day, inventing it on the spur of the moment. In return for certain favors he changed his life. He joined one of the groups. He had never been involved in any violence before. He liked it. He had a wretched existence to take revenge for. Today he operates in Guatemala City.

SAID THE DEFENSE MINISTER, Col. Arriaga Bosque: "*All* the subversion in Guatemala in recent years has come from Havana." But when secretary Rodolfo Gutiérrez of the government party in El Jícaro disappeared, kidnaped by civilians, his relatives didn't send a protest telegram to Fidel Castro. They went to the Defense Ministry itself. Col. Arriaga gave them a note to Colonel Carlos Arana, the commandant in Zacapa. Accompanied by a captain, Gutiérrez' family finally reached the village of La Palma in Rio Hondo. After an hour Gutiérrez was rescued from a concentration camp where the prisoners, before being murdered, are subjected to third-degree torture. In charge of the camp are more than a hundred well-armed civilians among whom are Hondurans, Cubans, and Puerto Ricans—exactly the sort of people whom the United States' Green Berets recruit for "work" south of the Rio Grande.

When engineer Montano Novella finally discovered the whereabouts of a vanished friend of his, he faced an armed guard at the entrance to the Zacapa village of Piñuelas. The guard consisted of civilians, landowners authorized to shoot to kill. Montano Novella obtained a *military safe-conduct* and was thus able to get his friend out of the camp where he was held. It was a return from hell: his friend described having seen two men castrated and a woman decapitated.

A journalist, Julio Edgar García, was threatened with death because—naming names—he disclosed in his paper, *El Gráfico*, a demonstration that the army organized in Gualán with members of a terrorist organization. That is the kind of information which may not be published in this country where, on the other hand, the press must give big headlines to "anonymous" expressions of "popular" support for the armed forces.* However, the Vice-President of the country makes a point of speaking clearly. Replying to a declaration by the students, the impetuous don Marroquín Rojas admitted it contained "some statements which are true," though he said that *not all* terrorist acts could be attributed to the army. In his view it was a case of legitimate defense. The Left started it, he said, and it was logical and proper that the Right should respond. "They use the same weapons in legitimate defense," he commented,

---

* "Soledad is the type who weeps blood," a friend said as he introduced me to a woman just out of jail. Her case illustrates the press freedom enjoyed by countries like Guatemala. At the beginning of November 1966, she had been arrested together with her husband. They were accused of having printed in their plant *one* edition of the students' paper. Fifteen men armed with machine guns converted their house into a war ruin, destroying all they could and incidentally stealing 1,300 quetzales (about $1,100 dollars). The two were in jail for several months without any proof of the charge being produced. The courts made no effort to solve the "crime." The prisoners were moved to another jail each time the press announced that they had been freed.

adding: "The army will not retreat in the struggle it is waging against Communism."

The brother of the guerrilla chief César Montes who had no part in the political struggle, was found dead, mangled by torture, three days after being arrested *by the army*. NOA took credit for the execution. The murder of relatives of revolutionaries, guilty merely of kinship, is now a routine phenomenon in Guatemala.

Tomás Guerrero was secretary of the Revolutionary Party —the government party—in Puerto Barrios. Privately and publicly he was a fervent anti-Communist. One morning in November 1966, he was kidnaped on the waterfront by a group of persons unknown. Some weeks later his body turned up somewhere, without the head. He had been the victim of a right-wing terrorist group. Meanwhile another leader of the same party, José María Rivera Flores, was pumped full of bullets by a military henchman in Chiquimula. A few days before they killed him, Rivera Flores, the party's local general secretary, had sent a note to President Méndez Montenegro accusing agents of the military in his district of organizing terrorism. The note, magically deflected from its addressee, came into the hands of the Defense Minister. Rivera Flores had signed his own death sentence. A week after they finished him off, Paulino Gutiérrez was found among some thickets in Olopa, cut to pieces with machetes. He too was prominent in the Revolutionary Party. Then a deputy, López Durán, made a speech in Congress demanding a stop to the attacks on his party comrades and naming some agents of the military as participants in clandestine terror groups. The Revolutionary Party—revolutionary in name only—promptly expelled him from its ranks for "lack of discipline." Soon afterward eleven leaders of the party in the Sanarate area, who had been arrested by the mobile military police, turned up dead in El Progreso. They had been shot and their faces burned to make them unrecognizable. Local people assert that the corpses were moved in a truck guarded by two army radio-patrolmen.

In *official* military reports these members of the *official* party were added to a list of four guerrilleros whom the army had surprised and killed.

Other Revolutionary Party victims have likewise been added to the list of "Communists" liquidated in the clean-up campaign: among them, a deputy who had been on the official delegation to the Punta del Este Presidents' Conference. From a Guatemalan military man's standpoint—Central American version of the Pentagon standpoint—a "Communist" is anyone whose ideas differ from those of a Guatemalan military man; more simply, anyone who has ideas. It is a crime merely to be young in some areas. Some men under thirty who left for Puerto Barrios to sell merchandise or collect accounts or make commercial deals were swallowed up in the ground. "Better not ask so many questions, . . ." their families are advised. Victims are picked on strict ideological lines. Informers, with faces masked, accompany the police along roads of the northeast pointing them out: "This one's a son of a bitch," "That one's a son of a bitch. . . ." Those thus accused disappear and nothing more is heard of them.*

Said an economics professor with whom I was discussing the country's balance-of-payments figures: "Expressing an opinion on Guatemala's problems nowadays is a way of signing one's own death warrant." Three bombs had gone off in his department. The dean had been threatened.†

---

* "Suicides" of military men also occur. Captain José León Pellecer García of the Zacapa army base killed himself, according to the official report, "by putting two shots through his thorax and one through his head." Someone rounded out the idea by adding: ". . . and carefully placed the gun on the night table."

† When I asked for an interview with Guatemala's top anthropologist, I received these lines via a mutual acquaintance: "Dear friend: I have received your kind invitation. Since I do not know what interest certain persons may have shown in you, I propose to take precautions. I will phone you in a few days. I will identify myself as *Licenciado* Rivas and you will invite me for a cup of coffee. I will suggest a time but not a place. At the time stated you will be at the corner of 13th Street and 10th Avenue, Zone 1. The bearer can describe me so you may recognize me. I will also be carrying a booklet in my right hand. O. K.? Yours, M."

The war of nerves, the atmosphere of panic, gives results. There are never any witnesses of a killing, even when people are dragged from their homes and shot down in the street. The families of many who disappear prefer not to take the matter to the authorities; relatives of jailed left-wingers ask the judge *not* to free them. Many university men have gone into exile. MANO threatened to kill the journalist McDonald Blanco if he won the elections in the Journalists' Association. He won. He had to resign.*

But terror is not always decisive. Jokingly, an intellectual whose life has been threatened more than once said to me: "As the Mexican song puts it—here, as in Guanajuato, life is worth nothing." He became serious and added: "My sister was very worried and came to see me because she knew I was on the 'lists.' But I said to her: 'Don't let it get you down.' If one has to face death for wanting a free Guatemala, well, one must face it. We're back again in 1810, eh? But in another way. Now Latin America is fighting for its second independence. And that's how a man shows he's a man—by whether he knows how to die when he has to die. What the hell. That's the way it is."

---

* Terrorist organizations take a particular interest in journalists. They know that if a newspaper reports that someone has been seized, this can sometimes save his life. A number of journalists have been threatened with death, and more than one case is known of journalists who have been kidnaped and tortured to make them tell what they know or can dream up about "Communist penetration" of the Guatemalan press.

A Premonition of Vietnam?

> *When the people began to be suspicious about the footprints, they gathered to discuss it and said: What can this be that sows death among the people, killing us one after the other?—Popol Vuh.*

ROCAEL, the guerrillero, is carefully cleaning his automatic as we talk. Suddenly, shading his eyes with his hand, he looks up at the slice of sky between the peaks: he seems to be looking for the helicopter which he has been describing to me: "The pal from Oreganal had ratted on us. We doused the fire we'd made for breakfast as soon as we heard the drone of the motor. The helicopter dropped six 20-pound bombs on us one after the other. We saved our skins by a miracle—there were very few of us and we could hide behind rocks: you should have seen those splinters flying every which way. Next day they dropped napalm. We were already off toward the west making for Teculután, and we saw the flames leaping up behind us. Man, how that brush burned! We saw it all from a distance of about three hundred yards, under fairly good cover in a ravine. An army light aircraft was dropping the stuff. The explosions were, you might say, softer than ordinary bombs. Some days later, in the Alejandría mountains near the Río Hondo, about eight of us in a patrol found five bodies, completely charred, in the vegetation consumed by the fire."

Vietnam is not the only place where napalm bombs are used. The United States has been lavish with the terrible jellied flame south of the Rio Grande. The Peruvian guerrillas were smashed in Mesa Pelada after a military campaign that included incineration of a small native village with all its inhabitants. Now they are using napalm in Colombia and Venezuela; in Guatemala they have been dropping it since the end of 1966 on guerrilla zones of influence. Stretches of trees and scrub have burned for three or four days; more than one peasant was a witness. The bombs go off like fireworks and a mass of brilliant red foam spreads over the mountains or runs along rivers destroying all it touches. Cedars and pines are burned down to the roots, animals are incinerated, the earth is scorched, rocks are blackened.

In an informal interview he gave me, the Vice President of Guatemala in person, don Clemente Marroquín Rojas, talked about napalm. It was easy to win his confidence, thanks to my providential likeness to a friend of his, a certain Newbery, who had been his companion in exile in Honduras thirty years before I was born. Half way through the conversation we both agreed that there are some things the North Americans shouldn't do in countries like Guatemala. "For example," he said, "they could have landed at the time of that Panama thing. Just landed." I agreed with deep conviction and, very cautiously, managed to discover what he was talking about. Thus I learned that a squadron of North American planes, piloted by North American flyers, had taken off from Panama, dropped North American napalm on a Guatemalan mountain, and returned to Panama without touching Guatemalan soil.

In his delirious newspaper *La Hora*, a few months before our interview, the same Marroquín Rojas had written a no less eloquent editorial: "The United States," he said, "would intervene in Guatemala if the Guatemalan army could not handle the problem. The 'domino theory' is also applicable to Guatemala. If Guatemala goes Communist, so will the other small countries around us." * And Senator Wayne Morse had

---

* To give the reader some idea of the pompous personality of Marroquín Rojas—a man with great influence over the military, who likes to take credit for every revolution and coup d'état that has occurred in Guatemala—I need only quote these paragraphs from one of his editorials:

"While Castro fills our countries with guerrilleros, Latin America may not

remarked that as the hemisphere knows, in Guatemala too the prospect of a civil upset can spark United States intervention.

It is a question of shadings: the Guatemalan Vice President and the United States Senator are both talking about "massive" intervention, implying an invasion in Dominican Republic style or a war like the one in Vietnam. Yet the intervention in Guatemala has been continuous and visible from 1954 to the present day. The CIA and Pentagon took power through the Castillo Armas invasion and never relinquished it. Today they exercise it through "advisers" crowding the government offices and ministries, and above all through the army and police, which move the levers of *real* power to the beat of the imperialist bandmaster. Terrorist groups, faithful copies of Vietnam "assassination teams," sow terror in Guatemala; as in Vietnam, napalm sets the mountains afire; the Green Berets say, as they once said in Vietnam, that "our mission is not to fight but to train." Yes, this sound and fury are familiar: Guatemala, like all Latin America, is a premonition of Vietnam; it is a country swarming with Rangers, Green Berets, and FBI and CIA agents.*

---

even give a gun to Cubans such as those who went to sacrifice themselves at the Bay of Pigs, where Kennedy committed the blackest of treacheries. Brazil, Venezuela, Peru, Colombia, and Guatemala, who could organize a revolution in Cuba do not attempt it, falling submissively in line behind Castro without a bleat or a bat of an eye, weeping like women for what they 'cannot defend like men.' It is true. A gesture, a stamp of the foot, anything to show a vigorous reaction. No, gentlemen, there is nothing; only tears, whimpers, and lamentations. . . . And the United States—everything in cash, money, loans, technicians who came to make us bigger cowards than we already were. . . .

"Do these cowardly peoples have the right to survive? No, gentlemen. They are peoples fit only for slavery, only to be menials. But not for fighting. Because the odd thing is that some people think the Cubans of today have one ball more than Batista had, and I insist they have the same two as every other man but are determined to make an upside-down cake of us small peoples who have been turned into whores by wealth, loafing, and ambition."

* It was learned, for example, that Richard Park Guthrie, John Charles Beckiman, Elton Nurmi, John Mess were assigned to the eastern Guatemalan military base of Jutiapa. Among those working in other army installations are Robert Bernestein, Arnold Blechenger, Oscar Hunter Adams, Edward Thorton Floyd, Arthur Kerr, James McNamara, Edward Suárez. Cuban counterrevolutionaries are involved in the systematic foreign military intervention

The guerrilleros take it for granted that "intervention by imperialism *on a large scale* will eventually come." That is, the present intervention will multiply several times in quantity and intensity. The Guatemalan army, whose corruption creates its own disintegration, is merely the immediate enemy; behind it waits the Pentagon itself. Guatemala's armed forces can fall to pieces some day, victims as much of their internal contradictions as of guerrilla action. But in contrast with Cuba, the flight of a Batista will this time be followed by North American invasion. César Montes, the FAR leader, put it this way to me: "Tactically we can't ignore the role that imperialism plays and will play here. We know that sooner or later the imperialists will intervene massively in Guatemala, with troops, as they did in the past in Nicaragua against Sandino, more recently against the Dominican Republic, and now in Vietnam. We figure North American intervention in our calculations for the fight, and this gives the guerrilla struggle a distinctive character."

It is in this framework that the Guatemalan guerrillas' contact with similar movements in other Latin American countries becomes decisive. That contact, which began with the Tricontinental Conference in Havana, is being successfully developed through organizations set up by the Conference. "Large-scale imperialist intervention will come one day. And then, well, we won't forget that Latin America is a unit. Then we'll have the right to admit revolutionaries of other countries into our ranks. Guatemala isn't the Dominican Republic, we're not surrounded by the sea, they can't isolate us; we have frontiers with Mexico, Salvador and Honduras."

A WHOLE FLOOR of Guatemala City's *Cruz Azul* building is occupied by North American "advisers" who run the national

---

against Guatemala: among others, Leo Rodríguez, a certain Besosa, and an individual known as "Papito." Also the former Venezuelan police chief Alí Lanzaeta.

police and participate directly in interrogating some political prisoners. These "advisers" operate behind the screen of AID (Agency for International Development), the instrument of the Alliance for Progress whose function in Guatemala is to supply the security forces with radios, patrol vehicles, and side arms. Under the command of Embassy military attachés, a large number of North American officials work in various sectors of the Guatemalan armed forces. Among the "advisers" actually with the army, not as mere witnesses but participants in military operations, Green Berets play a primary role. Counterguerrilla training is in their and the Rangers' hands. This training, which includes torture techniques and the organization of "assassination teams" as part of the "propaganda" job, is given not only in the United States and the Panama Canal Zone but also in Guatemala itself. According to the journalist Norman Gall, who has reason to know about it, *half* of all Guatemalan officers have taken counterguerrilla courses outside their country.

Under curious circumstances which would make a long story, I was able in Guatemala to get in touch with a deserter from the military police. Mario Julio Ruano Pinzón, who had been a sergeant at headquarters, thus described his own experience: "The Green Berets gave us special instructions for the counterguerrilla struggle in courses we attended on La Cajeta estate, somewhere in Zacapa. We were there from May to October of last year. They didn't let us go into town. We learned to survive in the mountains, the plants that you can eat, the water you can drink; they taught us to improvise bridges and cables to cross the deepest gorges. We also learned methods of killing, in mountain combats and in villages; how to disconnect those booby-trap bombs that blow up in your face when you open a door. Army intelligence officers gave us political instruction: they explained that Cubans were running the guerrillas in Guatemala. The Green Berets also taught us camouflage methods. With regard to prisoners, they advised us to kill them if we couldn't take them along. If they made a nuisance of themselves, we were told to finish them off on the spot. But not when they were leaders; then we had to get their names, take their papers, maps and weapons, handcuff them and take them to our superior officers. You don't kill leaders because they have to be interrogated first. The superior officers did the interrogating, not us."

Ruano Pinzón had just deserted from the army. He had his reasons. He is the only survivor of four soldiers, witnesses of a terrible massacre that no one will forget.

A day before the elections that made Julio César Méndez Montenegro President of Guatemala, twenty-eight revolutionary leaders were captured and disappeared. They were political, student, and trade union activists: Leonardo Castillo Flores, Victor Manuel Gutiérrez, Humberto Pineda, Fernando Arce Behrens, Francisco Amado, Carlos María Sosa, Juan de Dios Castillo, José Luis Meda, David Aguilar Mora, Victor Palacios, Marco Tulio Molina Licona, Carlos Enrique Galindo, Iris Yon Cerna, Ricardo Berganza, Rogelio Hidalgo, Mario Lemus, Emilio Vázquez, Marta Palacios, Eunice Campirán, Emma Judith Amézquita, and others. Their families could not find out where they were, living or dead, in which jail or in what ditch. Months passed and the guerrilleros obtained, by direct methods of pressure, promises from the Méndez Montenegro government to the effect that there would be an investigation. The investigation was never made. However, it was possible to discover what happened to some of the twenty-eight: Iris Yon Cerna, for example, the niece of Yon Sosa, had been beaten to death beside the Montagua river. It was also learned that most of the twenty-eight had been machine gunned in the armory of the Matamoros barracks and their bodies thrown into the Pacific.

The testimony of Ruano Pinzón confirms this. The following is what he told me in a secret interview somewhere in Guatemala City's suburbs. (One note of explanation: The man named Manuel, mentioned by Ruano Pinzón, was Victor Manuel Gutiérrez, the famous trade union leader who remains invincible in the memory of his people.)

There were four of us subordinates who went along with the officers as bodyguards that night. We were accompanying the Third Chief, Colonel Máximo Zepeda Martínez. I was on guard at the door when a light Ford truck drew up—I didn't see the license number—a green '58 model. They seemed to be bringing in the last bunch of prisoners. I asked a cop who was standing there and he said: "I don't know: there's a lot more inside." They were in the armory. I tried to go in but officers told me to stay outside. Colonel Zepeda looked at me and said: "Look, you'll have to sleep in the emergency room because it seems we'll be taking a trip out during the night." That's what he said to me and these three buddies who were with me—Carlos Leonardo, Lisandro Chacón, the other's name escapes me. Oh yes, Elías, Elías Dubón.

It was eleven-fifteen when Colonel Zepeda woke me up. He asked if we were ready. Before he told us to go and hit the hay Colonel Zepeda got a call from Colonel Arriaga Bosque who was the Vice Minister of Defense. The colonel told him to hurry up and get the job done. "Come here," said Colonel Zepeda to me. "Stand at the door and don't let anyone come in." The barracks phone operator, Miguel Angel Folgar, was a friend of mine and told me about the conversation. The prisoners were going to be killed right there in the armory of the Matamoros barracks. I said to him: "Those poor bastards sure are going to get hell." "You said it," he replied. "I heard Colonel Arriaga Bosque give the order on the phone."

I went up to one of the prisoners. He said his name was Manuel. I asked him why they brought him in and he said: "Politics." He said he used to work for Colonel Jacobo Arbenz. He asked me for a cigarette and I gave him one. The others didn't accept cigarettes and didn't say anything. Probably because of my uniform. I asked this Manuel if he wanted anything for his family and he said: "It's not worth bothering. We only have a few hours left." He said some day I would read some books he had written. He showed me how he'd been beaten when they arrested him. His back was all purple from blows with rifle-butts. I wanted to talk some more to them, but they didn't. Then the phone operator alerted me that the Vice Minister of Defense had phoned that he was coming over to the barracks. They were to wait for him. Colonel Arriaga Bosque arrived and went into a huddle with the officers. The colonel went in where the prisoners were and I don't know what was said because only officers were allowed in.

When they woke us up, Lieutenent Hugo Edmundo Alonzo ordered us to get some sacks that were there. We thought it was some routine thing and we started hoisting them into a pick-up and a jeep. When I hoisted the first sack I noticed blood on the sleeves of my uniform. I went to get the second and moved my hand over it and felt a face and a chest. "What's this?" I asked. "It's the guys they killed, get a move on," somebody answered. We all got covered with blood although they were wrapped in nylon. We went on hoisting.

"Who was in the armory when they killed the prisoners?" I asked Ruano Pinzón when he finished this story.

"When they were shot there were Colonel Zepeda, Colonel Oscar Ruiz, Lieutenant Hugo Alonzo and René Ortiz. Also Colonel Arriaga Bosque."

"Where did they take the sacks?"

It was eleven-thirty or twenty to twelve when we took off with the sacks from the barracks at 5th St. and 17th Avenue. Lieutenant Alonzo was in charge of the jeep and Colonel Zepeda of the pick-up. We drove to La Aurora airport. When we arrived I noticed that everything had been prepared. The vehicles flashed their lights and the gates were opened. We put them in a plane, the same guys that had put them in the vehicles. The officers didn't touch them. The plane was number 500 of the Air Force. Lieutenant Arena, who is now an Air Force pilot, was there. We hoisted the sacks on to the plane but we didn't throw them out. That was done by Lieutenant Alonzo, and some by Colonel Zepeda. We flew out over the Pacific to dump them. I don't remember how many sacks there were although somebody did mention it at the door of the armory. These people had been taken to the regular police, and when they brought them to the barracks it was obviously to shoot them, because they arrived all beaten up.

Three of the men who carried the bodies—Carlos Leonardo, Lisandro Chacón and Elías Dubón—died one after the other, eliminated, perhaps, by fate. One turned up stabbed in the *pensión* La Posada, another was shot in the back in a Zacapa cantina, the third was pumped with bullets in the Chiquis bar behind the central station. Ruano Pinzón escaped. As can be seen, he has weighty reasons for thinking that Rafael Arriaga Bosque, the Defense Minister, doesn't want those eyes and that voice to remain alive. His picture appeared in all the papers. They are looking for him.

IT WAS THANKS to napalm that the authorities found the buried corpse of Ronald Hornberger on the banks of the Teculután. The fire started down the river and swept along burning the banks; it exposed a rectangle of newly dug soil. The United States Embassy was helping actively in the search for him.

"Hornberger was a Green Beret veteran of the Vietnam war," César Montes tells me. "He came to us saying he was a reporter looking for material. He felt very secure. He was quite sure of his superiority over us. That was what gave him away. We talked to him, up in the mountains, for a few days. In a casual way he dropped some names and addresses in the city, and we had them checked a day or two later. None of these people knew him or had ever heard of him. He also lied about the place where he left his baggage. We checked there and it was false. Another funny thing that made us suspicious was that only the military aspects of our fight interested him, not our political motives for fighting; all his questions were very specialized on the military level. He had a complete line of fighting equipment and was a stellar performer with any weapon. He gave us exhibitions and said the hardware was a present for us. We sentenced him to death. Around his waist, under his shirt, he wore a nylon cord—the kind that Green Berets use to strangle people."

THE ARMY is the master of the situation in Guatemala. The military brass do not stop to knock on the door of Méndez Montenegro, who is constitutionally—but only constitutionally—their commander-in-chief. The upcoming budget must be slashed because the oligarchy won't pay taxes. The only untouchable appropriations are those of the Defense Ministry. The President is a virtual prisoner, but the military don't trust him and never did. Six weeks after Méndez Montenegro moved into the Government Palace, soldiers broke into the Olympic Stadium and opened up some cases which had been sent there by Presidential order. They found no arms, only jars of powdered milk for "social service."

Just as the army distrusts the President, the Pentagon—the major link in this chain of submission—distrusts the army. The local armed forces are inefficient and corrupt, with low morale and a glut of officers who are useless for fighting but good for plotting—one colonel for every thirty active men. The colonel may be illiterate, and almost all of the thirty men are young Indian peasants recruited by force. Officers involved in counterguerrilla operations get double pay, rewards, the right to booty and special vacations. The bodies of ordinary soldiers are rarely given to their families. The solid and close presence of North American military men has kept the Guatemalan army from collapsing before the guerrillas like a house of cards, and has incidentally served to stifle at least three coups d'état in the last two years.

North American "advice," like the Biblical tree, is known by its fruits. Not only have army and police officers and NCO's received special training, but "civil" groups directly dependent on the military and police forces have been trained by the United States outside the country. The Green Berets fit these groups out with weapons and ideas, and prepare them to fight in the "undeclared war" that imperialism is waging in Latin America.

According to confidential information of the government party's security organs, Guatemalan terrorist groups of the extreme Right have received military training just across the border in a little Honduran town near Santa Rosa Copán, which comes under the Honduran army's third military zone commander. "Accidents of geography": In April 1966, Gen. Robert W. Porter, Jr., chief of the United States Southern Command in Panama, told the Foreign Affairs Committee of Congress that North American engineers, together with some specialized officers, were engaged in a "civic action" program in the frontier zone where Honduran and Guatemalan troops have been making joint experiments in counterguerrilla warfare.

The armed forces' "civic action" plans consist not only of distributing powdered milk, medicines, and promises to villagers in areas subject to guerrilla influence, but also include intelligence operations often of a "dirty" type. All this is part of the "encircle and annihilate" campaign that the army has carried on against the guerrillas. Murder is blended with demagogy: while one hand kills people, the other distributes goodies. "You have to have a guerrilla unit nearby to get drinking water," said an Izabal peasant with a sense of humor. The north-to-south "combing" operation by three thousand soldiers in Zacapa in the first months of 1967 left much of the "propaganda" job in the hands of terrorist groups.

"Assassination teams" play exactly the same role in Vietnam as MANO, NOA and the other outfits play in Guatemala. Not merely the direct elimination of enemies; in Guatemala today, as in Vietnam, phony guerrilleros perform atrocities for the sole purpose of attributing them to the FAR. This is one of the lessons the Green Berets teach to their trainees. An exciting aura of mystery surrounds the Green Berets, the elite corps which cultivates the brotherhood of violence and the myths of living dangerously. According to the journalist Georgie Anne Geyer, the participation of a "small" group of these Eighth Special Forces men in the military training of Guatemalans has been officially admitted in Washington.

A person who has reason to know, and consequently to conceal his name, told me the following about torture methods used in Guatemala:

> They use various methods of torture. One consists of tying a thin rubber band around a man's throat, with its ends extending to left and right. Two individuals pull them, thus breaking the thyroid; to all intents and purposes the man is reduced to a sack of flesh and bones. He loses his voice, the ability to eat and to

make certain movements. There are a number of cases of this. One of them was Ricardo Martínez. Another, an old fellow of fifty-five or sixty who sold tomatoes in the Terminal Market in Guatemala City. One of the prisoners heard him groaning but he couldn't say a word. He conveyed by signs that he wanted to go to the bathroom but could neither stand up nor walk. I dragged him along and three days later he died as a result of the tortures.

There is one army unit, operating independently, that covers up these murders and the houses in the city where they are carried out. One of these places is behind La Aurora air field: a two-story house with an iron fence in front of it and all the windows filled in with building blocks. But it isn't the only one. They conceal these murders by throwing the bodies out on the highways, full of bullets.

Another torture method is tying the hands and putting a mask over the head filled with insecticide which they have to breathe. Many have died that way. Another was the one they used on the Pineda Longo brothers. One of them had his genitals cut off—that was the way his body was found. Some have had pins stuck in their eyes before being killed.

Those are the chief methods. In other cases they tie the hands tightly with wire or chains. Some bodies have been found with hands completely mutilated around the wrists. Another way of murdering people is to grab them right on the street and shoot them on the spot. That's what we call the "revolutionary hunt." They get hold of someone who knows people of the Left, any informer will do, and machine gun people they meet on the street.

With regard to the "advice" given by Green Berets in this department, an article by Donald Duncan, published by *Ramparts* of San Francisco in February 1966, is particularly eloquent. A few months earlier Donald Duncan, hero of the Special Forces and Vietnam war veteran, had left the North American army with his chest covered with decorations (he was the first Vietnam war soldier recommended for the Legion of Merit). In his explosive article entitled "The Whole Thing Was A Lie!" Duncan tells the following among much else:

Initially, training was aimed at having United States teams organize guerrilla movements in foreign countries. Emphasis was placed on the fact that guerrillas can't take prisoners. We were continuously told, "You don't have to kill them yourself—

let your indigenous counterpart do that." In a course entitled "Countermeasures to Hostile Interrogation," we were taught NKVD (Soviet Security) methods of torture to extract information. It became obvious that the title was only camouflage for teaching us "other" means of interrogation when time did not permit more sophisticated methods, for example, the old cold water—hot water treatment, or the delicate operation of lowering a man's testicles into a jeweler's vise. When we asked directly if we were being told to use these methods the answer was, "We can't tell you that. The Mothers of America wouldn't approve." This sarcastic hypocrisy was greeted with laughs. Our own military teaches these and even worse things to American soldiers. . . . I was later to witness firsthand the practice of turning prisoners over to ARVN for interrogation and the atrocities which ensued.

PROMINENT MEMBERS of Méndez Montenegro's government excuse the right-wing terror, which has piled up so many victims in the ranks of the so-called Revolutionary Party itself, by saying that it is no more than a reply to the previous challenge of Left terror. *Thus they forget that this long history of violence was begun by the U.S.A. in 1954, and that what is violent in the first place is the economic and social condition condemning so many Guatemalan children to death by starvation or disease.* But they also forget an essential difference. *History teaches its own lessons in the dialectic of hate: the President of the United States cannot wear the beard of Fidel Castro. The violence of the oppressor cannot be equated with the violence of the oppressed, although the Green Berets make their pupils learn by heart entire paragraphs of Mao Tse-tung and Che Guevara.*

There is no point in mechanically copying methods which, in any case, are different: the Left has never tortured anyone in Guatemala, nor taken vengeance against the families of its enemies, nor have the guerrillas ever killed their prisoners. The guerrilleros have not repeated the error of shooting point-blank at ordinary policemen or soldiers encountered on city streets. The Left prefers to attack those who give the orders rather than those who carry them out. When FAR or MR-13 sentence and kill a military chief or henchman in the course of the guerrilla struggle in the mountains or city, they explain the reasons in advance to the local population, and the peasants or citizens are aware anyhow, from their experience, that the condemned man had plenty of blood on his hands. On the other hand, when the right-wing terrorist groups sentence and kill a university student or a peasant suspected of rebelliousness, they inspire no popular outburst of joy for the elimination of a "Fidelista." The tactics of the counterguerrilla struggle are forced, in this sense, to start from the same basis as the guerrilla band itself: *the enemy is unpopular.* But in Guatemala as in Vietnam, the one who is unpopular is precisely the "friend" of the United States: big landlords and their administrators, greedy businessmen, the multiple elements of the army in city and country. Challenges and responses and more challenges and responses, the law of an eye for an eye and a tooth for a tooth—but on one side are the torturers, the murderers, the exploiters; on the other, the tortured and the victims, the exploited. A sigh of relief greeted the death of Colonel Enrique Trinidad Oliva, an ultra-reactionary officer, boss of a terrorist group, who had risen in the government in the wake of the Castillo Armas coup, and whose servility to Washington had earned him the nickname of "Gunga Din," legendary water-boy of the English. But a wave of indignation followed the next assassination: the Right decided to kill an Escuintla deputy, Carlos Siliézar, by way of reprisal. Siliézar had been elected by popular vote and was condemned by military resolution: an eloquent case.

Ex-Presidents or Traitors

> . . . and seeing that sunshine was coming,
> they told Vuch the Vulture to darken the
> morning, and he did it by opening his
> wings, and although four days dawned
> he darkened the sky four times by spread-
> ing his wings. Thus, today, if the vulture
> opens his wings when it is still dark, it is
> taken as a sign that dawn approaches.—
> Popol Vuh.

MÉNDEZ MONTENEGRO had promised agrarian reform. All he did was sign an authorization for landlords to carry arms—and they certainly use them against unarmed peasants. He had promised tax reform. It was the businessmen who finally decided who must pay taxes and how much—that is, no one and nothing. He threatened to limit profits, to cover the deficit in the budget; he ended by cutting salaries of government employees. An American tragedy: south of the Rio Grande, presidents who take office through more or less free elections, intending to launch a program of more or less superficial reforms, *soon become traitors or ex-presidents.*

It is well said that power is like a violin—one picks it up with the left hand and plays it with the right. These are the conditions for survival: to assure twenty-five years of bigger profits and full guarantees to the imperialist concerns that plunder Chile of its copper, lowering their taxes as they extract more wealth from the country and leave it less of a future; not to touch the interests of Standard Oil and U.S. Steel in Venezuela; to dress up the underdevelopment of Peru with the bright raiment of technocratic "solutions"; to use the memory of the Mexican revolution to govern against its principles; to destroy the economy of Uruguay so it will serve only to repay debts with new debts, chaining the country and its future to foreign banks.

The incumbent President of Guatemala is a prisoner of the same alternative. His own country's experience shows him that as soon as anyone *really* tries to change the structures of submission and backwardness anywhere in Latin America, the military brass of the moment appears at his back, sword in hand. Civilian committees for Defense of Democracy are formed; the CIA and FBI mobilize their agents. Trained by and for the Pentagon in the United States or Panama, with North American manuals, doctrines, weapons, and support, Latin America's generals are ready to sink their teeth into the "internal enemy." They are hardly installed in power when they invade the universities of Brasilia or Buenos Aires and express with clubs and bullets their natural distrust of any activity of the human brain. White House "liberals" raise no aesthetic objections to this.

The most efficient dictators are so gross and vulgar that all they don't know would make an encyclopedia—and no small one. But the imperialists have their own reasons for feeling comfortable. *All* the military men who have become Presidents in these recent years—in the Dominican Republic, Ecuador, Brazil, Bolivia—are the product of the Pentagon's "re-structuring" of Latin American armies. They are men trained and equipped under the United States military aid program, called Alliance for Progress Security, precisely in order to move against any civil regime that might want to make a reality of Alliance for Progress principles and its program of timid reforms. Certainly neither Arbenz, nor Bosch, nor Arosemena, nor Goulart, nor Paz Estenssoro had in mind the socialization of the means of production and exchange. Some tried to start an agrarian reform, distributing privately owned lands with indemnities to expropriated landlords. Others simply committed the error of thinking that their hungry populations deserved more attention than active coupon-clippers in Wall Street.*

SANTO DOMINGO

IT IS AN unequal contest in the Dominican Republic in 1965: Coca-Cola bottles filled with naphtha against the dictator-ship's Sherman tanks. At the approach to the bridge, the peo-ple fight baring their breasts to the bullets. The defeat of a General Wessin y Wessin, known as "the jackal," seems cer-tain. Then the Marines land. Washington has sent them to protect the lives of North American citizens on the island. In a few days there are 40,000 Marines and not a single North American remains to have his life protected—although there are still many Dominican citizens to have their lives sup-pressed. The Marines reverse the situation.

The Constitutionalists, who had raised the banner of re-turning Bosch to power—the democratically elected Presi-dent who was overthrown by vote of the military—fight from roofs and sewers, in patios and lanes. It is hopeless. With Caamaño's forces cornered between the Ozama river and the Caribbean, resistance becomes impossible. Tears of impotence and fury, clenched fists; all the young blood has been shed to no purpose. The foreign occupation forces control the "elec-tions," which take place in a climate of terror. The winner—Balaguer, the right-hand man of the United States' old gang-ster associate Trujillo, who still holds world records for mas-sacres and tortures during 32 years of dictatorship.

Bosch is flown back into exile. In 1963 his constitutional regime had lasted a few months. During his brief term he, who believed in the Alliance for Progress, could not even find out

---

* Chilean President Eduardo Frei has been able to operate with much broader scope than the others. In a sense he is an exception, to the extent that he can carry out some reforms in sectors where imperial interests will not be hurt: for example, land redistribution and education and housing plans. Here the alternative to the so-called "revolution in liberty" is not a "gorilla" govern-ment à la Onganía or Castelo, but rather the million votes won by the Left in 1964.

what happened to the "aid" funds; nor could he realize even one of his timid reform plans. He was overthrown by a coup d'état set in motion by the North American military mission in Santo Domingo. Later he would bitterly denounce the United States as being able to get along, in Latin America, only with governments of "pirates with Cadillacs" or military butchers like Trujillo.

ECUADOR AND BRAZIL

IN THESE YEARS other joys have been vouchsafed to the northern imperialists by the countries south of the Rio Grande. On a July night in 1963, President Carlos Julio Arosemena of Ecuador, an aristocratic and jovial banker, "talked too much" after a banquet in honor of Grace Lines at which the United States Ambassador, Mr. Maurice Birnbaum, was also present. Tuned up by the drinks, Arosemena loudly recalled certain unpleasant information about the economic exploitation suffered by his country at the hands of Grace and some other foreign concerns. Not many hours passed before the military tossed him out of the Presidency, accusing him of being "soft on Communism" and of having visited Moscow.

On the last day of March 1964, the Goulart government fell. By chance in the following week I came upon a wall in the Rio de Janeiro suburbs with a placard defining the event: "*Enough of intermediaries!*" said the crudely scrawled inscription: "*In the next elections, Lincoln Gordon for President!*" The good Lincoln was then United States Ambassador in Brazil. The cable of congratulations from Lyndon Johnson to the conspirators had reached the capital *before* the provisional President was sworn in. One could understand the haste. Goulart had decided to put a tourniquet on the bleeding of dollars that ails Brazil because foreign concerns operate like suction-pumps on the national wealth. He had defied the international coffee trust (which ten years before had compelled President Vargas to blow out his brains with a bullet). He had announced a timid and controversial agrarian reform and voting rights for illiterates. His education and housing projects, too, were within the "spirit" of the Alliance for Progress.

But it is generals and ambassadors who make our history, not "spirits." Castelo Branco emerged to give the green light to North American capital, which took over Brazilian industry, distraining it for debt or buying the shares for a few centavos by telephone. Suffocated by the violent tightening of internal credit and the fall of mass consumer demand, businesses could only retain their "national" names and sometimes not even that. The biggest factories, including petrochemicals, fell into foreign hands, protected by the new guarantee agreement for foreign investment; Electric Bond & Share got the scandalous "indemnity" it was demanding, and the Hanna Corporation picked up practically as a gift the richest iron deposits in the world—with railroad and port thrown in.

The national football team stopped wearing red shirts, by express order of the authorities a week after the coup. Now one can hear even the "Bossa Nova" sung in English. A United States Defense Secretary once remarked that what is good for General Motors is good for the United States. The formula was sagely rounded out by one of Castelo Branco's ministers: "What is good for the United States is good for Brazil."

The saga of plunder rolls on. In the last century Portugal drained Brazil's rich deposits of gold for the benefit of England. In a few more years Brazil will have no manganese, a basic mineral for making steel. Whole mountains of its territory are being shipped to the United States and have been for some time. The Costa e Silva regime continues conceding to imperialist concerns vast areas of Brazil, containing fabulous wealth in the form of strategic minerals and precious stones; the Amazon is the new "Far West" for North American "pioneers." Under these conditions it mattered little to the "anti-Communists" that Castelo should negotiate and obtain substantial financial aid from the Soviet Union, the benefits of which are now enjoyed by his heir, another general. Peaceful coexistence also feeds on these touching examples of collaboration between the great powers.

AT THE END of 1964 Paz Estenssoro fell in Bolivia. He himself later said that the coup had been planned in the North American military mission in La Paz, by a certain colonel who was worried by the President's hesitancy in permitting the army to enter the mining centers, and by the commitments he had obtained from de Gaulle and Tito to finance some development projects. Yet he could never obtain North American aid to finance national smelters for the "devil's metal," tin, which Bolivia exports in crude form, at a loss, to the United States and Britain. None of the "international" credit organizations, managed from Washington, ever paid any attention to this Bolivian demand. And as prices for raw materials fall on world markets, a country that does not industrialize is a country condemned.

Paz was a proven friend of the United States and had broken relations with Cuba. But the Pentagon decided to install one of its favorite wolf-pups, General Barrientos, in power. General Curtis LeMay was especially devoted to Barrientos. The story goes that on one of Barrientos' many trips to the United States, some time ago, the wife of a high Pentagon official drank his health at a party with the comment: "*But see how American he looks . . .*" (she meant *North* American). Barrientos does his best to deserve the compliment. He had denationalized his country with great enthusiasm. This "Steve Canyon of the Andes" is responsible for the massacre of miners in mid-1965, a bloodletting repeated on St. John's Night in 1967. The dynamite thrown by the miners of Siglo Veinte, Huanuni, and Catavi, and the old rifles given them by the revolution of 1952, were of no avail. Rangers, special parachute troops and infantry surrounded the mines while aircraft sprayed machine-gun bullets and bombs. Soldiers forced the doors of houses,

shooting blindly at families. "Order" was established. Today
the miners can continue dying before they reach thirty, destroyed by silicosis, but one must suppose that they are happy.
They have been saved from "Communism."

ARGENTINA

DESPITE some early frictions, now overcome, the United States
has the best of relations with General Onganía's regime in
Argentina. This grim cavalry officer had hardly settled into
Rivadavia's chair* before he dissolved the political parties,
proclaimed himself the absolute power, and stormed the University and some trade unions. He is imposing by force a socio-
economic policy which the constitutional regime of ex-President Illía could not apply without some restraint and at tortoise
pace, committed as it was to the electorate.

Having elected himself, Onganía need render accounts to
no one. He can cut the workers' living standards and unload on
to them the weight of the crisis, and lavish benefactions with
impunity on the big export and foreign concerns whose investments now have more facilities than the State itself; they are
"feeling very much at home." Before making arrangements to
turn over the oil and gas industries, denationalize public services, and sabotage the national steel industry, Onganía had
already co-authored the "ideological frontier" thesis with the
present President of Brazil, General Costa e Silva. They both
affirmed that United States intervention in the Dominican
Republic was a good example to follow, since the fight against
"Communism" requires shelving of the old concept of "sovereignty." This idea, as seductive for large countries as it is
dangerous for small ones, is the basis of the present competition between Argentina and Brazil. While the venerable Illía
hesitated, Brazil took the lead by sending troops to Santo
Domingo and one of Castelo Branco's generals took command
of the "inter-American" occupation force. But Argentina is

---

* Bernardo Rivadavia, first president of Argentina (1826).—*Translator.*

regaining ground, and it still remains to be seen who will chalk up the most merits in administering and defending North American interests in the south.

THE SPIRIT OF THE ALLIANCE FOR PROGRESS

THE SIXTH BIRTHDAY of the Alliance for Progress was a mournful celebration. The United States Senate cut its appropriation from $650 to $578 million, which would be used—as in previous years—for buying North American products at the world's highest prices, to put powdered milk, blankets, and promises in the hands of Latin America's oligarchical governments. In 1966 the United States spent more than 40 Alliances for Progress on killing Vietnamese. Johnson spoke with sincerity at the sad festivities: "If anyone asks if the Alliance is a success, we may well reply that only our sons or grandsons will know if it is a success." Latin Americans do not have to wait that long to know it is a fiasco.

Instead of deeds, words. The rhetoric of revolution replaces revolution. What is a reality for the Left becomes a shield for the Right. The White House continues proclaiming the need for deep changes in Latin America, the "revolution of growing hope" of which Kennedy sang. The language was presumably poetic but became flagrantly tasteless in the mouth of his successor. Lyndon Johnson from Texas announced that "we will make" in Latin America "a revolution of sweat rather than one of blood and tears." He pointed with pride to the fact that in 1967 "no government in this hemisphere has been taken by force." He really meant to say that nothing turned up in 1967 to make the State Department feel it had to overthrow anyone. But who is going to be fooled by this prostitution of language? That which is affirmed in words is negated by deeds. What has the present "American dream" of an all-gorilla continent to do with the text of the Alliance?

The only "basic reform" proposed in the Alliance for Progress Charter was agrarian reform. It is significant that the only country to have carried it out in these recent times should be the "accursed" one, banished from the Organization of American States shortly after the Alliance was born. Cuba, in fact, is the sole exception, and has made its revolution *against* imperialism and not thanks to it. We see a double paradox when we bear in mind that the Alliance had a clear political meaning from the outset. It was Washington's response to the challenge of Fidel Castro, setting Democracy in economic competition with Communism. Events have shown that imperialism and local oligarchies prefer to compete on another level.

Significantly, the Alliance was launched just when a "special military program to guarantee Latin America's internal security against subversion" was being presented to the United States Congress. The "subversion" was pinpointed without delay in just those countries whose governments proposed to introduce undeniably necessary reforms. All of the governments genuinely seeking to act "in the spirit of the Alliance" had a short life.

It is prohibited to act but permitted to talk. No one denies Méndez Montenegro, President of Guatemala, the right to proclaim reforms which he will not make.

The Unpunished Crimes of Poverty

> *Your pride of rank shall be cut down. . . .*
> *You shall occupy yourselves only with*
> *making pots, pans and stones for grinding*
> *corn. Only the children of the scrublands*
> *and desert shall speak with you.—Popol*
> *Vuh.*

THE DEPARTMENT OF STATE openly supports Méndez Montenegro. The Embassy, directly or indirectly, heads off a coup d'état every three months. The President survives as a prisoner, because his impotence makes him completely innocuous from the standpoint of the political and economic interests for which North America is the world watchdog. Guatemala gets credits to sustain the national currency and a few jars of powdered milk fall straight out of the sky into the peasants' hands. Imperialism seeks to alleviate with one hand the consequences of what it does with the other. Meanwhile the constant threat of a coup is effective blackmail to immobilize the President or push him into treason. Yesterday, Arturo Frondizi understood this very well in Argentina.

Today everything in Guatemala is done and undone in the name of the fight against "Communist aggression." But isolating the guerrillas while their cause remains unconquered is like plowing the ocean. The rebels in the mountains are not the product of Cuban caprice, but of the order of things that condemns most Guatemalans to misery and humiliation, to premature death. Those who oppose changes, guardians of a social structure which makes it so easy to die and so hard to live, apply democratic methods of terror to save the system.

Chaos is created, performing two functions. It provides pre-
texts for a possible coup d'état, which for the moment the U.S.
government deems unnecessary and inopportune. At the same
time it exonerates the military from responsibility for the dirti-
est part of the clean-up job, for it is under a civil regime that
indiscriminate repression has been let loose.

Méndez Montenegro stands condemned. History will not
judge him for what he does but for what he does *not* do, or for
what he allows the real enemies of Guatemala's development
and liberation to do. If he decided to act, some colonel could
accuse him, pressing a bayonet to his breast, of inability to
control the violence which the same colonel has organized.

SOON AFTER his victory in the last elections, the incumbent
President of Guatemala asked a group of wealthy men:
"Which do you prefer, gentlemen? To have a hundred *quetzales* in your pocket with uneasiness and insecurity, or to have
seventy-five fully guaranteed?" He was thus defining his government's intentions: that the rich should be slightly less rich so
that the poor could be slightly less poor. One might say that
his proposed changes were not excessive. He took over the
government in mid-1966. Today the rich are still getting richer
and social tensions grow, because three-fourths of the population receive a daily income of twenty cents—and living costs
are as high as in the United States. Rapid population growth
and the cruel inequalities of income distribution make the
average Guatemalan poorer than he was a decade ago—when
he was *very* poor—despite the country's economic development.

The per capita income in Guatemala is one twenty-fifth
that of the United States.* But this statistic only assumes its
true dramatic dimension when one bears in mind that for a

---

* In his *Realidad jurídica del indígena guatemalteco*, Julio Hernández Si-
fontes states that many Guatemalans receive a daily income of eight cents.
Official figures give an average total income of forty cents a day per capita; the
average for three-quarters of the population is twenty cents a day. These are
centavos of the quetzal which is currently worth about 85 cents.

handful of Guatemalans to be able to live like kings, protected with their privileged families behind the high walls of their mansion-fortresses, eight of every ten persons have to be illiterate and go barefoot and eat a third of what they need. According to calculations made by Professor Alfonso Bauer Paíz, 97 percent of Guatemalans will be illiterate by the year 2,000 if present demographic trends continue and present structures remain intact.

To illustrate the life of the landlord oligarchy, a few paragraphs from a report of the Inter-American Agricultural Development Committee (CIDA) will suffice.* Say the CIDA technicians:

> The upper class live in the capital. Of 12 large estates studied in the west of the country, it was found that 11 of the owners lived in Guatemala City. . . . The major part of this landlord group has higher and university education and many of them have studied abroad; they often send their sons to be educated in the United States and Europe. . . . They seek to maintain a life of colonial aristocracy, while at the same time trying to idealize and imitate the North American standard of living. They have a big house, with many servants, luxury automobiles (the interview on one estate was delayed an hour because the owner had not yet arrived in his bi-motor plane), modern domestic appliances, etc.; at the same time they frequent social centers distinguished by their high cost, and keep up to date with the fashions. . . . They frequently travel abroad and have a marked tendency to internationalize their social relations. . . .
>
> Like investors of any Latin American country, those who are economically strongest invest in land for purposes of speculation.
>
> In two cases of estates on the Pacific slope, it was found that the owners would not allow agricultural extension agents to enter . . . they imagine that if they permit entry to these agents, or frequent visits in general for purposes of technical aid or agricultural experimentation, such visitors will arrive with other intentions having nothing or little to do with agriculture. . . . At the national level, these landlords do not realize that they harm the country with their constant demands for credits which would

---

* See Appendix I for fuller text of this report.

benefit other sectors of production, and with their policy of sending abroad the annual dividends from their operations.

The report also makes these observations about the workers:

It may be said that rural workers are in an economic and social
situation which imposes apparently insuperable limitations on
them. Furthermore we can confirm that the rural workers' situation has worsened in recent years. Since as matters stand no job
alternatives exist for these persons, they are increasingly dependent on the estates where they work, which at the same time
worsens their contractual relations with the employers. Thus a
common statement by those interviewed was that if for one reason or another they do not show up for work, part of the wages
owed to them is withheld, and they cannot complain because
they would then be fired.

As to the future, the workers generally state that they have no
hope of bettering their lot, nor is there anyone to whom they can
turn with their problems except the local authorities (mayors,
judges etc.); however, the general position is that they go to no
one because nothing happens anyway, especially when the said
authorities are related to the employer.

Asked in what way they would like to improve the situation,
46 percent of the interviewed workers said they wanted more
land or a bit of land to call their own, and the remaining 54 percent said they preferred higher wages; but they realized that
under present circumstances they have no way of asking for it,
lacking any organization for the defense of their interests.

Latifundio, minifundio, rich land, poor people: the *minifundio* does not yield enough to live, so the man who owns or
rents it sells his labor to the *latifundio* for a pauper's wage.
There are still many sharecroppers paying rent for their land in
labor or products. Twenty-two estates have an average of
23,000 hectares each, the best lands in the country: in some of
them only six or seven percent of the area is cultivated. There
is a total of six agronomists and thirty-four threshing machines
for more than a half million Indian families who work the
little sunbaked plots on the western heights.* The official cen-

---

* By the latest available figures Guatemala has 74,269 farms of 0.34 hectares
each: two percent of all proprietors own 72.2 percent of the total land. The
next census will no doubt reflect an even greater concentration of land

sus gives the figure of 750 tractors in the whole country. Those same figures show that the *latifundio* exploits less than thirty percent of its land. No roads exist in Alta Verapaz along which trucks or even carts can pass. The big farm-owners do not need them: it is cheaper to transport the coffee on an Indian's back. In the countryside drinking water, electric light, and latrines are unknown.

Guatemala is short at least a million housing units, and there is one doctor for each 5,400 inhabitants; in Quiché Department, one doctor for each 120,000. Hospitals, beds, medicines are lacking. (Yet Guatemala is one of the seven Latin American countries occupying a "place of honor" in the State Department for having "joined with the United States in aid to South Vietnam by sending medicines.")

The unpunished crimes of poverty: of every 1,000 children born alive in this country, 120 die before the age of four, according to official data which are kept comfortably on the low side. Of those who don't die, nearly all are condemned to survive without schools or shoes or Sundays or toys. This violence of the system, condemning so many children to die of disease or hunger, is even more terrible than that of the extreme-right terrorists. Even without the echo of one shot being heard, Guatemala would still—like all Latin America—be a battlefield on which death wins.

JUST OFF the plane in Guatemala, and queueing up for the customs officials, I overheard two North American citizens beefing strenuously about the new government. They looked like businessmen and no doubt were. They said that Guatemala today is a "tax hell." Later I realized they were referring

---

ownership: every day more land passes into the hands of fewer people. The process of plundering small proprietors takes on ever more dramatic characteristics. To cite but one example, the Camalmapa farm in San Miguel Chicaj, Baja Verapaz, was parceled out some years ago by the National Institute of Agrarian Transformation. The neighboring big landlords seized the peasants' crops, or burned them. Some peasants spent six months in jail for the crime of having no title to land which the state had given them.

to certain feeble brakes which are applied to the flight of foreign exchange by way of profit remittances—a small tax that
was imposed some years back and is now beginning to be collected—and a limit to spending abroad by tourists. Everyone
predicts a short life for this tax, confident that dollars will
soon take wing as freely as ever without even the smallest in-
convenience. And as for the limit on spending, anyone can
make any number of trips abroad, to the Mexican frontier or
some equally remote spot, taking along $2,500 on each occa-
sion for each member of his party. One need only produce
some letter to show that it is a "business trip," and further
controls vanish. For "tourist expenses"—an easy pretext for
the flight of dollars—Guatemala bled to the tune of $24 mil-
lion in 1966, twice as much as three years earlier; and more
than $22 million left the country in remittances of profits on
investments. The exporters, for their part, can peacefully leave
their dollar earnings in New York banks—without Guatemalan controls or taxes.

Guatemala is one of the three countries in America where
least taxes are paid. Tax collection was only 7.3 percent of the
domestic product. And the owners of land and businesses, who
take full advantage of the numerous forms of tax relief, are
"untouchable." We have only to glance at the 1967 budget:
taxes do not provide enough to cover expenditures, which are
much larger. But of the $119 million collected annually, only
$17 million are direct taxes on income and property, and the
remaining $102 million are unloaded on the consumer masses.
The present government's Secretary of the Treasury sought to
increase taxes and modify the scale so that those who have
more would pay a little more, those who have less a little less.
The income tax—which in any case most enterprises avoided
paying—was to be slightly raised; the same North American
capital which pays nothing in Guatemala is subject to very
high taxes in its own country. The Secretary's project freed
from obligations the owners of plots of land so small as only to
provide hunger rations for those who work them. Also, there

was to be a sliding tax-scale on land, with a maximum of *one percent* for the big *latifundio*. "It's a Communist project," "the Secretary is a Communist," "a Communist plot": no need to wait for the reaction. The daily press trembled with fury, "private enterprise" raised its indignant voice, and in Congress the opposition to the project was headed . . . *by a deputy of the government party itself*. A military coup d'état was seen as inevitable. Finally the President decided that the Chamber of Industry should draw up the definitive tax plan. The tide of wrath waned and the flood waters subsided. The big landlords, however, are not completely satisfied, although today the largest haciendas pay taxes of *six per thousand* (six-tenths of one percent!) on landed property.

In the same way the reform of the industrial development law was shelved and the Labor Ministry's steps to enforce the minimum wage were halted. Thus, too, the Ministry of Agriculture could act with impunity against hundreds of thousands of small wheat growers in the high plateau—honest, hard-working Indians who, however, lacked money or military (that is, political) influence. And thus the promises of agrarian reform were also wiped out. During my stay in Guatemala the courts forced the government to give back one of the few farms it had expropriated. The official plan to distribute "state lands" among cooperatives and peasants—which did not even scratch the power of the big landlords—was publicly denounced by the Vice President of the Republic himself, don Clemente Marroquín Rojas, who wrote in his newspaper *La Hora*: "This agrarian reform is a Communist plank. . . ." The army is making its own "agrarian reform" experiments in the Petén. It aims simply to transfer to these uninhabited forests all the defects of rigidly class-divided Guatemalan society. It is building the foundations there for future *minifundios* and *latifundios*.

The pressure of landless peasants is felt all through the country. In the land distribution in Nueva Concepción, the Castillo Armas dictatorship settled 2,000 families whom the regime itself had evicted from other lands. There, 18,000 new families had sprung up (according to a census made on the spot) by 1958, and today there are more than 30,000. As in all of Latin America, the *latifundio* sends unemployed labor into the cities. Guatemala City expands like an oil slick, new suburbs mushroom, new people keep flowing in.* But job opportunities are no better, as anyone can see. Swarms of shoeshiners will fight over your oxfords in the plazas, many hands will be thrust forward to open and shut the door of your car, and you will not walk two steps without being offered lottery tickets, newspapers, fruit, soft drinks, *tortillas*, "souvenirs of Guatemala."

ALTHOUGH it makes vague claims of continuing the revolutionary cycle of Arévalo and Arbenz, the Revolutionary Party—the party of the government—has in its ranks people of the most varied ideas and interests. Its present leaders have completely lost sight of the progenitors whom they claim and exploit politically. Through successive internal "purges" it has changed into another party of the system without any distinguishing feature. By 1963 it was already one of two organizations applauding the reactionary coup of Peralta Azurdia, sharing this honor with Castillo Armas' party. Today it is from the Revolutionary Party that the first objections arise to any proposal the President may support to tackle the causes of Guatemala's prevailing social injustice. Méndez Montenegro is alone with his impotence. He sees the best elements and ideas of his party going down to defeat with the complicity—by commission or omission—of those who run it. In his newspaper the Vice President, who applauded the CIA invasion in 1954, daily attacks the President in blunt terms, calling more or less openly for a coup d'état. A pugnacious, turbulent, slick politician, constantly churning out thoughts and literary

---

* According to a report by a special Municipality commission, the population of the marginal areas, living in hovels around the city, grows by ten percent per year.

compositions, Marroquín Rojas lives in a perpetual state of agitation. "The man whom the times demand has not arisen. We must seek him out, we must create him," he proclaims, and warns: "Something is rotten in Denmark and some surprise could occur . . . this manoeuver could end in suicide." He says they want to kill him to eliminate him from the government because he tried to push Méndez Montenegro forward; but it's hopeless, he says, and now there is nothing to be done: "I have met with dark resistance proceeding from I don't know where. . . ."

Homage from the Rotary Club or the Lions, photographers' flashes pop, the President smiles. Photos also show him smiling as he lays the foundation stone of some new rural school: but they also permit a glimpse of a revolver butt at his waist. A smile of triumph? Méndez Montenegro "triumphs" by transforming himself into his own enemy and placing himself at the service of forces he once fought. He was one of the lads who lit the first spark of the 1944 revolution, when the Guard of Honor barracks was attacked. His present fiasco, as sad as it is inevitable, has a definite value. It serves to convince many simple people of the simple truth which the guerrilla incarnates and propagates: that in Guatemala land and liberty can be won only by violence. For this reason, too, the great majority of the armed Left is made up of peasants.

Anatomy of Submission

*There was sky and there was earth, but
the light of the sun and of the moon was
dulled. Then one named Vucub Caquix
became arrogant because of the wealth
he possessed.—Popol Vuh.*

On one of the first days of 1967, in an office on Pine Street,
in southern Manhattan, the face of Abraham Weber turned
scarlet. He was furious. "I'm not going to let a little Central
American country impose its will on an American company,
understand?" he shouted. At that moment his visitor, the
Guatemalan Carlos Rafael López Estrada, decided he had had
enough and ceased to be the lawyer for IRCA, International
Railways of Central America. IRCA had belonged to the
United Fruit Company until a New York court applied the
anti-trust law and ordered the company to unload its shares.
After some magical prestidigitation, during which United
Fruit's multi-million-dollar debts to small shareholders disap-
peared, the railroads ended up under control of Abraham
Weber and Louis Yaeger, North American capitalists. The
change benefited Guatemala in no way whatsoever.

These foreign railroads, the only ones the country has, seem
like something out of a documentary about the Mexican
Revolution of 1910. Old and stertorous and by now useless,
they give the worst imaginable service. They pay no tax—
even though carts and bicycles pay taxes in Guatemala. The
railroads do not even pay for postage stamps. The State has
renounced the right to check their account books. IRCA says

it loses money. Whatever IRCA says is accepted as revealed truth—in spite of some fleeting and fruitless "intervention." The wrath of Mr. Weber against Guatemala can be explained: Lawyer López had proposed some cautious changes in the situation "to give the government the feeling that its sovereignty is recognized," as he himself explained it to me later in his office.

Phantom figures, double or triple bookkeeping, millions made and lost in the twinkling of an eye: in Latin America, nations fail to understand themselves by failing to understand the devices of the firms that dominate them. The little disguised digits keep growing. Like modern art, it is more what they suggest than what they say. Foreign companies' account books are sacred. Who can question the declared value of their holdings, the stated total of their profits?

BACK IN 1857 the Guatemalan foreign ministry, approving the plan for a Latin American congress to be held in Lima, suggested that "it would be curious if the United States, from which we get the disease, should also furnish the remedy." Sadly, the phrase retains its reality. In these last years the avalanche of new North American capital into Guatemala has sharpened the country's sufferings instead of lightening them. Imperialist exploitation has been diversified. The United Fruit Company is no longer absolute lord of the land. But that does not mean that the economy has been diversified in the way its delayed development requires.

Legally the situation of United Fruit has not changed. The 1924 contracts, which gave it part of Zacapa Department and all of Izabal, remain in force. Its other branch, the Companía Agrícola de Guatemala, continues enjoying the privileges of the contract of 1936, which remains in force till the year 2000. United Fruit still owns the harbor at Puerto Barrios on the Atlantic. But there is now another port in Guatemala, the company no longer owns the railroad, and the cable agency, Tropical Radio, was acquired by the government. Guatemalan front-men or important ex-officials of United Fruit now work in the Pacific-bordering lands which belonged to the Compañía Agrícola. It is they who plant cotton and raise cattle; the firm no longer operates directly.

The new owners, most of them purely nominal, have relied on financing by local banks to "acquire" the lands; North American banks have also extended credits to finance these operations. United Fruit has announced that it will buy the banana production of "independent" planters. At the same time a government campaign insists on the need to rehabilitate the country's traditional banana production, now clearly in decline.

Thus the "banana republic" image has changed. The imperialist system of exploitation that victimizes it has a new face. The agreement guaranteeing foreign investments, the industrial development laws, and the new perspectives opened by Central American economic integration have made Guatemala an even more attractive sanctuary than before for capital coming from abroad. The firms pay no taxes, dizzily multiply their earnings, are assured of free return of profits in dollars to the head offices, and make use of *Guatemalan* savings which the Bank of America channels for their benefit.

THE INVESTMENT guarantee agreement, born of Castillo Armas' government and ratified by Ydígoras Fuentes, provides that disputes between the Guatemalan state and a foreign concern—problems arising from expropriation, nationalization, the setting of exchange rates or exchange control—are not within the competency of national courts. They come under an arbitration court which may or may not have Guatemalan representation and which, in any case, must be numerically dominated by non-Guatemalan arbiters. In the event that the national currency (quetzal) cannot be freely and equally converted into dollars, the United States government will pay the investor the amount of the investment at his valuation, and will automatically become Guatemala's creditor for an equivalent sum. The Guatemalan government grants the North American government all the rights of a private investor. Thus the Bank of Guatemala must pay in dollars the sum total of investments at the companies' valuations, although these may be completely imaginary, whenever the companies decide to withdraw from the country. If this is not done, the amount will be added to Guatemala's foreign debt under the agreement.

In cases of expropriation, the United States government will pay in dollars whatever sum the expropriated party claims as indemnity. Here too the North American government will become Guatemala's creditor. To put it briefly, government-to-government negotiation or country-to-country debt replaces the relation between a government and a private firm. The Bank of Guatemala's Economic Studies Department has rightly noted that the agreement is not only incompatible with prevailing legislation, but contradicts "the present tendency of all countries to accept foreign capital on the basis that it submit to national law and never invoke a foreign government's protection."

Other Latin American governments, however, have signed guarantee agreements which look like carbon copies of what the Guatemalan dictatorship signed. One recalls the ominous text of the agreement with which Castelo Branco consummated the sellout of Brazil. If the United States were to organize a contest of indignity and obsequiousness in Palm Beach, the jury's heads would ache deciding on a winner among so many serious Latin American aspirants.

The guarantee agreement would be the first obstacle to any government trying to promote Guatemala's independent development. It is there to protect the dreams of the monopolies which control electricity, railroads, sea communications, great tracts of land, and basic industries, the mainsprings of trade and banking.

Foreign capital endows itself with a messianic function. Hired technicians and writers assure us that, thanks to its magical properties, poor countries are in a position to emerge from underdevelopment.

Rafael Piedrasanta, dean of Guatemala's Faculty of Economic Sciences, noted in an article on foreign investments in Guatemala:

- that foreign investments have been coming into Third World countries for a long time, and that the problems, rather than shrinking, have become enormous;
- that the investors live abroad and feel no identity with the countries where they put their capital: these are no more than sources of profit. In Guatemala's case, many owners of firms there do not even know the country—the profits are remitted to them wherever they live;
- that foreign investments in Guatemala have been badly oriented, toward industries that are not basic;
- that in Guatemala these industries pay no taxes, employ little labor, and generally work with imported raw materials, in addition to importing intermediary products needed for the manufacturing process;
- that Guatemala does not even get the benefit of lower prices: gasoline refined in the country costs the same as if it were imported;
- that foreign investment displaces and asphyxiates national capital.

I was myself able to collect enough confidential information to provide many examples. I choose one: Kern's fruit and tomato juice plant. In 1960 Kern's brought into Guatemala $800 in foreign exchange, and used machinery which, together with the patent, it valued at $200,000. Six years later Kern's had multiplied its capitalization tenfold, with capital of $3 million and plenty of "local" credit. Capitalization of profits was registered as a new investment in dollars, so that whenever it likes the firm can demand of the Bank of Guatemala, in the name of those original $800 and a few old machines, the millions of dollars produced by Guatemalan workers, consumers, and savings-account holders. Kern's has sold its plant to the Grace Co., now also owner of the Ducal canning plant which was started with national capital. The Grace Co. owns Guatemala's most important Pacific coast port and monopolizes maritime transport through Grace Lines. Other Central American enterprises started with national capital have ended up in its hands: Pozuelos, the cookie plant in Costa Rica, and Optimo, which produces instant coffee in Nicaragua.

Free competition with hens is an old dream of the fox in every hen-coop on earth. In Central America small handicraft workshops of less than five persons occupy sixty percent of the total labor force. The *really* national enterprises are very weak. What can Salvadoran and Guatemalan cookie-makers do when a foreign firm takes over Pozuelos? Wait their turn: they will be gobbled up. Guatemala's delicious Taxisco cheese, made in the old Spanish style, cannot compete with "standard" North American cheeses—surplus products which, like powdered milk, arrive to ruin national producers under the pretext of "aid"—and which, incidentally, also ruin the taste of the consumers.

THE ALLIANCE for Progress—that is, the United States—supervises credits given by the Banco Centroamericano, although the Bank's capital is partially formed by the countries of the area themselves. Industries of the "economic integration" are born and boosted at the whim of foreign investment, not in the national or regional interest.* A good part of the Inter-

---

* Under the Central American economic integration treaty, the basic purpose of the Banco Centroamericano is "to promote through credit, security, and direct participation in public and private investments, the balanced economic development of Central American countries. To fulfill its objectives the Bank has its own capital of $16,000,000 contributed by member states and the income from loans and trust funds." An idea of how the Bank performs the functions for which it was created may be obtained from some of the stipulations, cited below, of the loan agreement with *Alimentos Kern's de Guatemala* whose sacrifices for the country we have described. The loan is from the Alliance for Progress, channeled through the Bank in the name of the Agency for International Development. The contract was signed July 17, 1964, and the following is part of the communication sent by the bank to the company:

"*Section* 5.06.—Goods to be purchased with dollar funds of the loan shall

American Development Bank's capital also originates from
Latin America, but its credits are channeled by the United
States in directions convenient for *North American* export
needs.

"Factories" arise in Central America which simply mix
products imported from the United States. They get the Banco
Centroamericano's financial support without effort. Guatemala merely adds distilled water in the manufacture of per-
fumes and cosmetics—and very little labor. The investments
that arrive to "industrialize" the country tie it more than ever
to foreign industry. In 1966 Guatemala paid out $80 million
on service of debt, mostly to finance imports—more than twice
as much as the previous year. "Everything comes from
abroad," an economist remarked to me. "Our import needs
have grown enormously. We buy from the United States far
more than we sell to it; we depend on the United States for

---

originate only in the United States or the five (5) countries of Central
America.

"*Section 5.07.*—Goods purchased with dollar loans shall be transported only
in ships of the United States, Central America or any other country of the
world with the following exceptions: Union of Soviet Socialist Republics,
Albania, Bulgaria, Checoslovakia [*sic*], East Germany, Hungary, Rumania,
Estonia, Latvia, Lithuania [*not included in the USSR?*], Poland, Danzing
[*sic*], North Vietnam, Continental China and other areas controlled by Communism [*sic, sic*], Outer Mongolia, and Cuba.

"It is also stipulated that the cost of shipping such goods may only be
defrayed if these shall have been transported by ships under the flag of the
United States, except when it shall have been otherwise agreed in writing with
AID.

"*Section 5.08.*—Maritime insurance shall be financed provided that the insurance be obtained at the lowest competitive rate and provided that no discrimination by statute, decree, law or legislation exist in the Central American
countries against any marine insurance company authorized to carry on business
in any state of the United States of North America. [*It is not specified what is
meant by "discrimination."*]

"*Section 6.05.*—Establishes that the Bank is obliged to facilitate visits to
your plant by the AID so that this organism can confirm that the project's
financing has been carried out in accordance with the terms of the contract."

The Banco Centroamericano utilizes the services of Price, Waterhouse &
Co., instead of giving work to Central American professionals. Thus, this firm,
which operates *illegally* in Guatemala, according to evidence provided in a
report to the Society of Economists, audits the accounts of the Banco Centroamericano and the Grace Company.

buying and selling. The trade-balance deficit is covered by credits which also come from the United States." He added, shaking his head: "If it weren't for the credits, the government would fall." Incidentally, seventy-five percent of the trade-balance deficit arises from trade between Guatemala and the United States and Canada.

The credits increase the imbalance. They are the lifebelts grabbed by the government of Méndez Montenegro, the same Méndez Montenegro who said soon after taking office: "Today the public debt is enormous. It has reached the limit that the country can stand."

Like all loans received by Latin American countries, the credits that Guatemala obtains from "international" organs like the Banco Interamericano, the International Bank for Reconstruction and Development (IBRD) or the Export-Import Bank come with *conditions*. Marvels of the Alliance for Progress: the Agency for International Development extends credits imposing the obligation to buy North American materials, transported in North American ships, insured by North American firms with payments through North American banks —all at prices higher than the world market. The technicians are North American—the most expensive in the world—and also the controls (the armies are not alone in having foreign "advisers"). On the Alliance's books, loans to finance "foreign supervision" appear as "aid" to Guatemala. Thus the country goes into debt to renounce its right to choose. For Guatemala *does not choose*. Like all of Latin America, it has been deprived of the right to decide from whom it buys, what it buys and at what price, what development projects it must undertake with what technicians, and what industries must be established on its soil.

The Alliance reveals itself to be a device to consolidate United States politico-economic dominion over Latin America. The most important loan received by Guatemala's present government is the one extended by the IBRD for the Jurún-Marinalá hydroelectric project. The IBRD imposed on Guatemala a "gentleman's agreement" with Electric Bond & Share, and recognition of the British debt of 1827(!) which was canceled in the days of Ubico. New bonds appeared like rabbits from a hat, and the Grace Co. is their most important promoter. The "gentleman's agreement" implies payment to the North American monopoly of a fat sum in *indemnity* for damage they might suffer in a river-basin which Castillo Armas had given them *as a present,* and for possible loss of profits from the development of a national source of electric power.

Loss of profits? The electric power will be supplied to Electric Bond & Share; the state commits itself to guarantee that the firm will not be hampered in its profitable business of *distributing* the energy—so profitable that *the firm itself arbitrarily fixes the price of electricity.* If the government does not pay the indemnity that Bond & Share imposed, and if it does not guarantee a "free hand" for the firm's business, it doesn't receive the "aid"—which in any case it will have to pay for with interest.

This same Jurún-Marinalá hydroelectric project, now the subject of a shameful agreement which has not been made public, was to have been undertaken by the Arbenz government without begging for foreign capital or eating any corporation's humble pie. Arbenz fell in 1954. At that time Guatemala did not owe one centavo abroad; today, payments for amortization and interest on debts devour a third of the country's exports. The government can well feel proud of this loan, so publicized and at the same time so secret.*

Prior to 1954 the government controlled the export of coffee. Today it limits itself to paying the fines when firms

---

* There is no written record of the most humiliating conditions imposed by IBRD on the Guatemalan government. Nevertheless the contract itself, drawn up and approved in English, includes such conditions as this: ". . . the INDE (National Electrification Institute) will not acquire or initiate the construction of any other installation for generation, transmission, or distribution of electrical energy unless it shall have established, to the satisfaction of the Bank, the technical and economic viability of said installations and shall have adopted a financing plan acceptable to the Bank." In other words, Guatemala subordinates its future energy policies to the pleasure of a foreign bank.

sell contraband coffee beyond the quota fixed by international agreement. Guatemala is a prisoner of the international network of interests that handles trade in basic products.

Like all Latin American countries it takes a severe beating when the price of its main article of export drops. *In 1965 Guatemala received the same amount of dollars for its coffee exports as in 1956, although it sold fifty percent more.* Thus in those ten years production grew to no purpose. The figures become much more significant when one bears in mind that when prices of raw materials and foodstuffs exported by poor countries fall, they rise in the same proportion for the machinery, semi-manufactured and finished goods imported from rich countries.

A slump in the price of coffee is a catastrophe for Guatemala. The country has not diversified its production, and certainly North American perfume and fruit-juice factories are not going to compensate for the loss. Foreign capital is not interested in developing basic industries which could give the country independent strength. Standard Oil lets the oil lie untouched in its immense deposits by way of reserve; no one exploits the rich deposits of iron ore in the east; the chemical industry has not even been born, although its potential is enormous; sulphur and lead depend on the will and pleasure of foreign firms, which are happy to ship them out of the country but not to put them at the service of its development.* Guatemala has an enormous shortage of energy despite its fabulous water-power resources.

In such a weak country only the state could set all this dormant wealth in motion for the national benefit.† But in

---

* The extension of the port of Matías de Gálvez, decided by the present government, is for the benefit of Exmibal, North American firm which exploits the nickel of Izabal as it previously exploited the nickel of Cuba. Construction of the Morales-Izabal highway serves the same purpose.

† The development of cotton production in Guatemala, touted as a great contribution to the country's progress by "private enterprise," is the result of action by INFOP, a state agency created in Arévalo's time to develop production. INFOP took over the risk of some investment necessary to economic development, promoting among other things the cultivation of cotton—which

Central America the state performs a purely decorative function; it is "judge and policeman" in suppressing popular rebelliousness by fire and sword, but in the economic field it plays a weak, diffuse, or worthless role. The United States, which grew beneath the shelter of a rigidly protectionist government policy—with internal subsidies and strong tariff barriers—and went through the decisive experience of the "New Deal," discourages state intervention in the economy in Latin-America: the "know-how" of *its* monopolies decides everything.

So the North American ambassador to the OAS, Sol Linowitz, could afford the luxury of the smug comment that the United States is rich and Latin-America poor for "reasons of heritage and culture."

---

the Indians were already planting before the Conquest. The state contributed land, the initial capital, wages, fertilizers, and insecticides, and undertook to absorb the losses. The first planters received half of the earnings without any investment. Subsequently, cotton planting continued to be encouraged by a policy of government loans; the government obliged industrialists to consume national cotton, and also fixed the prices, throughout the revolutionary decade.

Betrayal and Promise in
Latin America

*And the tree gave forth its sap and it
flowed red into the cup.—Popol Vuh.*

ALTHOUGH Méndez Montenegro's "constitutional" regime
lends a mask to the ruling military dictatorship in Guatemala,
the country sums up with tragic clarity the situation in Latin
America as a whole. Events in Guatemala provide a pulse by
which to feel Latin America's long tortured history, with all
the weight of its defeats and the strength of its hopes.

In Guatemala things are more easily seen and felt than elsewhere. This is a regime that violently imposes the law of
survival of the strongest; this is a society that condemns most
people to live as if in a concentration camp; this is an occupied
country where the imperium shows and uses its claws and
teeth. Dreams inevitably fade into nightmares and one can no
longer love without hating, fight for life without killing, say
Yes without also implying a cry of *No*.

Here the enemy is not made of smoke. Imperialism here is
not merely a secret hand manipulating prices on international
markets, buying and selling stocks on the New York Exchange,
investing capital and extending loans to give it dividends and
sovereignty. Here imperialism is all of this plus napalm burning the mountains and Green Berets teaching murder and
torture; it is a flesh-and-blood businessman or ambassador imposing his will on a minister or a president, a law that is
mocked and a peasant who is swindled, a young student riddled
with bullets in the streets. Here imperialism is also its own
negation: guerrilleros reclaiming with arms in hand the right
of Guatemalans to govern themselves.

Guerrilla violence is the reply to the system's violence. The double violence of the system: *indirect violence,* expressed in Latin America by the simple but terrible fact that each year as many children die of hunger or disease as the toll of three Hiroshima-type atomic bombs, and *direct violence* by the military and police.

Official statistics—the grim figures cited more than once in this book—themselves tell about the *indirect violence.* But these figures fall short of the reality. Officially, for example, 71 percent of Guatemalans are illiterate; but let us see what the Inter-American Agricultural Development Committee (CIDA)—the offspring of the Alliance for Progress which I cite extensively in Appendix I of this book—has to say about that: "In our researches carried out in Quezaltenango, Totonicapán and Sololá, of 161 persons studied 121 said they were illiterate, or 75 percent. Of the remaining 40, 11 could barely read and the others did not grasp what they read: hence they could not be called fully literate. . . . Many of the persons studied said they had been to school, but had done no reading nor writing since and had completely forgotten what they learned."

The system *imposes* ignorance on the workers it exploits, as a suitable complement to poverty. The hands of the majority produce the wealth of the minority. Why permit those many heads to learn to think? If the rich estate-owner is to spend his summers in Miami and a North American citizen is to get his coffee for a dime, the Guatemalan plantation worker must resemble as nearly as possible a beast of burden. What would happen if he knew that he is what he is by the choice of others and not by his own cursed fate?

Revolt would happen. The revolt that is already happening, because experience teaches its wisdom also to men who can neither read nor write. That revolt is answered by *direct violence,* uninterrupted since foreign military intervention overthrew the government that gave Guatemalans the first consciousness of their dignity. The above-mentioned Inter-Ameri-

can Committee—certainly not made up of revolutionaries—
notes the example of a mini-landowner dispossessed by the
Castillo Armas "liberation." "Under Decree 900," says the
CIDA, "he was granted a small piece of land and credits to
work it. Filled with enthusiasm, he threw in his own savings
(over 90 quetzales) to cultivate the land. Some time later he
was arrested for the crime of being an 'agrarian reformer,' and
the former owners of his plot destroyed his crops. He then
had to take refuge in the mountains. Now (1963) the Banco
Agrario is demanding payment of the loan plus nine years of
interest, and since he cannot pay he is being prosecuted."

Decree 900, promulgated by Arbenz, was the only serious
attempt at agrarian reform in Guatemalan history. The military dictatorships that followed the fall of the revolution have
violently consolidated the power of the *latifundio*, which com-
pensates with starvation wages for the fall of world market
prices resulting from imperialist exploitation. Peasants without land, cheap labor bought for a few pennies. The army, the
police and their terrorist bands torture, jail, and murder so
that "democracy" may continue exhibiting its virtues "in
peace."

THE INFORMATION in this short book suffices to confirm that
North American intervention in Guatemala, since 1954, is as
continuous as it is demonstrable. Today that intervention assumes determinate forms which already portend its future
intensification.

Nevertheless the struggle goes on against the Guatemalan
army, *which substitutes for the Marines as an occupation army
against its own country. Thus it is still not a case of an Algeria
or a Vietnam*, where the wars of liberation had or have a
foreign army as the enemy, where a French policeman or a
North American soldier incarnates without any disguise the
foreign power against whose oppression the country fights.
The fact that North American military intervention in Guatemala has not yet taken on massive proportions makes it harder

for some to understand the national and patriotic character of the guerrilla struggle: the fight is still against men who speak the same language, live on the same soil under the same sky, even if they are the armed force of a foreign power.

The guerrilla, focus of tension which sharpens and brings to light the system's contradictions, is not unaware of the dialectic relation between challenges and responses. As the conflict deepens and broadens, the possibility of open imperialist intervention grows; but with such massive intervention the possibilities also grow for a popular revolution, backed by an ample majority and under the banner of national resistance against the foreign invader. *Bringing the contradictions to red-heat is thus the only way to make imperialism tear off its mask,* once the local army "doing its work" in its interests is defeated.

Nor is the guerrilla unaware that *institutionalized oppression can become a habit.* "Constitutional" sanctification of a military dictatorship—now a familiar phenomenon in other countries—confuses matters in the eyes of world opinion and even of some sectors of society in Guatemala itself, who see in Méndez Montenegro a civil president whom it is neither possible nor desirable to resist by the same methods used against dictator Peralta Azurdia. The guerrillas, then, cause the contradictions to explode *before* they are consolidated.* But no one expects victory the day after tomorrow.

The guerrillas are quite aware that the Cuban experience will not be repeated in the same terms in which it occurred there. Revolution is *not* imminent: the guerrillas are not living

---

* The Costa e Silva regime in Brazil has been more *simpático* than that of despotic Marshal Castelo Branco. In this second phase the dictatorship can vaunt a certain "liberalism"; there are light modifications of economic and foreign policies, and broader relations with the trade unions are pointed to with pride. Relations also improve with both the "permitted" opposition and a good part of what had apparently been banned. This becomes possible because there is almost nothing Brazilian left to surrender to the United States: gradual restoration of "democracy" will seal the country's final defeat. General Onganía himself admits the possibility of a second phase in Argentina, the "political" stage of the "Revolution" which he heads: it will happen when Argentina has been completely denationalized.

on the eve of the final apocalypse, but are betting on a long-
term revolution, "a process, not a happening," the final outcome of a series of painful, difficult, but possible conquests.
The "false alarm" that made many think the Cuban revolution would promptly light revolutionary fires throughout Latin
America is but sound and fury for those who keep their arms
at the ready in this stage of the continental historical process.
The revolution proceeds on its thorny upward march *in spite
of* the dreamers who confused it with a fast weekend outing.

On this road, paved with more disappointments than rewards, there is no turning back. Bridges are burned once and
for all, in full knowledge that hope will always be less possible
than despair.

The Guatemalan guerrilla movement, seasoned by several
years of struggle and with many advances and retreats in its
book of experience, is made up of men purified and defined by
violence. "The people must wage revolutionary war since their
enemies will not renounce violence," said the Rebel Armed
Forces, replying to an amnesty offer made by this government,
a government born of a pact with the former dictatorship.
The guerrilleros rejected the amnesty ("fighting for the revolution is not a crime but a duty," said César Montes to me),
although they agreed to suspend military operations on condition there would be no repressive moves against the people.
Very soon afterward the army let loose its biggest offensive.

The choice is made in advance. The revolutionary merely assumes the alternatives posed by the system, between one violence and the other: resignation to the other side's violence
or legitimate use of his own violence. A guerrilla movement
does not conspire from basements; nor can it permit itself the
luxury, like some traditional Left parties, of acting as if it
were a Salvation Army which, in addition to passing the collection plate, issues communiqués.

For a guerrilla force, survival is the best and most conclusive
evidence of popularity. In Cuba, when counter-revolutionary
guerrillas appeared in the Escambray, Fidel Castro's govern-

ment organized and armed 50,000 peasants who undertook to clean out the mountains in a few months. Why doesn't the Guatemalan government use this method? Why don't Leoni in Venezuela, Lleras Restrepo in Colombia use it? Do the guerrillas keep going because Cuba supplies them with arms, men and money? The counter-revolutionary guerrillas in the Escambray were supplied and sustained by the biggest power on earth. It was the people that sealed their fate.

Deeply rooted in the peasantry, proudly linked to the best in their country's history, Guatemala's guerrillas are the product of betrayals and promises, crimes and hopes, which were not of their creation but which have summoned them to the quest of the keys to the stormy future.

APPENDICES

The Murderer Extols His Victim's Virtues

The following, without the change of a comma and omitting only the statistical tables, is part of a commentary on "reforms in the 1944–1954 period." It is taken from a book entitled Land Tenure and Socio-economic Development of the Agricultural Sector in Guatemala, *produced by the Inter-American Agricultural Development Committee (CIDA). CIDA forms part of the OAS (Organization of American States) and was created on the same day that the Punta del Este Charter was approved, when the Alliance for Progress saw the light. This work, of irreproachable origin from the standpoint of the most democratic "democrats," was published in 1965 by the Pan-American Union, General Secretariat of the OAS, Washington, D.C. In 1954 this same OAS gave its blessing to the annihilation of the experience which today, by way of delayed post mortem, its technicians eulogize with predictable but meaningless qualifications.*

THIS PERIOD was characterized by the execution of many measures to renew the country's socio-economic structure, agrarian reform being among the principal ones. The bases of the agrarian reform were set forth in the 1945 Constitution, which specifically proscribed the *latifundio*, permitted expropriation of private property for the public benefit, after payment of indemnities, and stipulated that it was a primary function of the State to promote industrial and agricultural development.

A decree of Ubico, obliging all men to work two weeks a year on the roads, was suppressed. Also officially abolished was a practice existing in one or another form since the colonial era: that is, the obligation of forced labor on coffee plantations for Indians cultivating less than two hectares.

In 1945 the "Ley de Titulación Supletoria" was enacted, dealing with the protection of ownership of land by those who had cultivated it continuously for not less than ten years without legal title. In the same year, now under the Presidency of don Juan José Arévalo, the first national agricultural colony was organized in Poptún, El Petén Department.

Subsequently the government sought to help tenants and farm employees by protecting them in their relations with the big landlords. Thus in 1947 the Labor Code was promulgated, specifying and regulating the rights of workers laid down in the Constitution; that is, trade union organization and the legal right to strike. The formation of unions on big plantations was encouraged, permitting the workers to demand better living conditions. However, the Code barred peasant unionization on estates with less than 300 workers, which constituted a brake on better relations between employers and employees in parts of the country.

On the other hand it was decreed in 1949 that all estate owners and all State farms must continue renting lands for two more years to those who had held them as tenants during the past four years. Legislation was also passed compelling landlords to rent out idle lands, stipulating as a condition of the lease that no more than five percent of the value of the product obtained could be charged. This was called the Law of Compulsory Rental, under which idle lands must be used, and at the same time tenants were protected against landlords' abuses.

The Law of Compulsory Rental did not, however, give all the hoped-for results, since it was mainly applied to properties that were already rented rather than to those containing unused land. Furthermore the big estates were not generally rented, which is not surprising since renting of land was prevalent among middle farmers, especially in the eastern part of the country. For that reason the law mainly affected this group of farmers, tending to destroy a series of established customs which regulated tenant-landlord relations with respect to tenancy and exploitation of the soil. But wherever this law was applied it directly affected both employers and workers, causing enormous resentment among the former. Outside of this, there is no other important legislation for Guatemalan agriculture in the period 1944–1952, although the traditional distribution of lands to communities and individuals continued at a slow rhythm.

In 1951 Colonel Jacobo Arbenz, who had promised to push agrarian reform, assumed the Presidency of the Republic. The Agrarian Reform Law, also known as Decree 900, was approved by Congress on June 17, 1952. Its basic proposals, almost all expressed in the law's first three articles, were: eliminate feudal-type property in the countryside; abolish backward forms of production relations, especially forced labor and relics of slavery such as the *encomiendas* of Indians;* give lands to agricultural workers who have none or very little; provide means of production and the technical aid necessary to improve methods of exploitation: expand agricultural credit to be available for all farmers, etc. In this way old forms of production would be replaced by others which would prepare the way for industrialization of Guatemala. The law included a series of arrangements to achieve the above objectives; many of these were certainly appropriate to the conditions of the country, although others gave the impression of aiming to concentrate control of the land in the government's hands.

The law provided for expropriation of idle lands; of those not under cultivation either directly or on the owner's behalf; of those rented out in any form; of municipal lands under

---
* Colonial assignment of Indians to a lord.—*Translator.*

certain conditions; and of lands necessary to form urban populations. However, existing ownership of estates up to two *caballerías* (90 hectares) was respected, whether cultivated or not; and even of larger estates if they were rationally used. The same would apply to lands of the Indian communities and privately owned and rented lands used for commercial crops such as coffee, cotton, bananas, sugar cane, beans, cereals etc., and also to forest reserves.

Lands would be granted to peasants, tenant farmers, and farm workers on a lifetime usufruct, lease, or property basis according to the case. To determine how much land would be granted, various factors would be taken into account, but in general small family or multi-family plots were given, with the exception of Petén cattle lands which would be larger.

Lands to be distributed among the beneficiaries were: (a) lands expropriated from individuals, (b) national lands and (c) national farms in production (expropriated from Germans during World War II). There were varying opinions in Guatemala about the method of dividing up government plantations raising commercial crops, as for example coffee, since these farms could be more productive when worked as a single unit, and above all because the peasants would not know how to operate alone; production might decline and there was the risk that they might use them for subsistence crops. Nevertheless national farms were the first lands distributed, in lots of 5 to 25 *manzanas* (3.5 to 17.5 hectares), according to their state of exploitation and their quality; but titles remained in the state's hands and the beneficiaries received only lifetime usufruct, for which they paid three percent annually of the value of what they produced.

All beneficiaries of agrarian reform would have to pay for lands received; payments would be made annually and would consist of a small percentage of the land's annual production, during a determined number of years and according to the type of beneficiary. Beneficiaries of lands which had been expropriated in favor of the state would receive them in lifetime usufruct and pay the government three percent annually on the value of the crop. On the other hand workers for whose own benefit lands were expropriated would receive them in permanent ownership, paying five percent of the crop value annually for them. The payments collected would go to the National Agrarian Department. The Law also stipulated that deeded lands could not be transferred nor mortgaged for twenty-five years; and, with respect to beneficiaries on a usufruct basis, they would lose their rights to the land if they stopped cultivating it for two years. In both cases renting of the land to third parties would be allowed.

In addition to beneficiaries covered by the Law in general, and as long as lands were still available, any person, farmer or not, who had capital to exploit them would have the right to rent nationalized lands. The limitations, in this case, were that not more than 400 *manzanas* (280 hectares) per person could be leased, and that the periods of lease would be not less than five nor more than twenty-five years, renewable at the end of any period. The maximum basis of tenancy was fixed at five percent of annual production, and subleasing was prohibited.

Expropriated lands would be paid for with agrarian bonds, guaranteed by the government, at three percent annual interest and with amortization over periods varying up to twenty-five years. For this a ten-million-quetzal bond issue was floated. With regard to the valuation of expropriated lands, this would be the same value that had been declared for land-tax purposes, as recorded in the property registers in May 1952.

To give technical assistance to beneficiaries, and for the supply of cattle, seeds, implements etc. by the government, part of the annual collections from persons favored by the reform under various headings would be used.

A fundamental aspect of the program would have to be financing the new farmers, for which the Law proposed to establish a Bank. The National Agrarian Bank, as it was called, was founded in July 1953, and began functioning the same year. It was a state entity of autonomous character, whose primary and specific object was to extend credits to small peasants and thus complement the agrarian reform. It was set up with a capital of 10,520,000 quetzales; possible deficits during the first five years would be covered by the state. The Bank's forms of operation were subject to standards that would lend flexibility to its operations, always based on experience.

Finally it was decided to create an organization to apply and administer everything connected with the reform. This was the National Agrarian Department, coming directly under the President of the Republic who in turn assumed immediate responsibility for the whole agrarian reform program. It was clearly stipulated that the President's decisions would be final, thus canceling the right of *amparo** in cases of disputes on application of the law. Apart from the above-mentioned, the National Agrarian Council, departmental agrarian commissions and local committees on the municipal level were charged with executing the law.

Application of the law began immediately and at an accelerating rhythm. Any person who believed himself eligible to receive land could specify lands which he considered subject to expropriation, and the same could be done by National Agrarian Department officials. Claims were made before the local committees, which within three days must inspect the lands and prepare a report; if expropriation was indicated, this was recommended to the Departmental commission; the commission in turn transmitted it to the National Agrarian Council, which made the final decision.

When the law had been in force and applied for two years, the state had available for those needing land 603,615 hectares expropriated from individuals and some 280,000 hectares of national farm lands, a total of 883,615 hectares (1,263,860 *manzanas*). Distributed on an average of 7 hectares (10 *manzanas*) per worker, up to 126,000 peasants could have been benefited.

---

* In Latin America, a writ obtained from a judge protecting an individual against a specific legal procedure by the government.—*Translator*.

In a period of 18 months, from January 1953 to June 1954, 1,002 farms totaling 1,091,073 hectares were declared to be affected by the Agrarian Reform Law; of these, 55 percent were expropriated and 8,345,545 quetzales were paid for them in indemnities. In one month alone, February 1954, more than 100,000 hectares were expropriated.

To pay for the expropriations, the Banco de Guatemala up to June 1954 issued 7,870,775.00 quetzales in agricultural bonds on the authorized total of ten million quetzales. This shows that the issue of bonds for indemnities closely followed the rhythm of expropriations.

The number of peasants actually benefiting by the reform is estimated at about 100,000. After the change of government, there was apparently a process of destroying records of the application of Decree 900. Of this number some 30,000 were workers on national farms, among whom 101 farms, including their extensions, were distributed. Seventy farms were distributed in the form of small parcels; twenty-nine were given in the form of cooperatives, and two in mixed form as parcels and cooperatives. Other information sources mention different figures: for example, the office of Agrarian Affairs, in 1958, gave the figure of 88,000 beneficiaries of whom 23,000 were national farm workers. In fact, exact statistics are impossible, due to the speed with which land distribution was undertaken and the state of general confusion into which the country fell toward the end of the Arbenz government; thus the figures given should be taken with reserve.

In the field of agricultural credit the achievements were no less notable than in the distribution of land. Before the National Agrarian Bank began its operations, credit assistance to beneficiaries of the reform began through the Banco de Crédito Hipotecario Nacional. From March 1953 to June 1954 this bank had carried on business with 160 farm units, extending 17,843 loans to cooperatives and recipients of individual plots, for a total of 3,371,185.10 quetzales of which 3,049,-

091.97 quetzales—90 percent of the value of the loans—had been recovered by July 1954.

The National Agrarian Bank began its operations in October 1953; in less than two months it had branches in Mazatenango, Cobán, Chiquimula and Quezaltenango in addition to its central offices. In the course of November and December 1953, the National Agrarian Bank extended 986 loans for a total of 122,012 quetzales, and during the first six months of 1954—the season when preparations for sowing are made in Guatemala—it granted 35,000 loans for a total of 8,388,234.40 quetzales. Of that amount 87.4 percent went to agrarian reform beneficiaries, and the remainder to small producers who had never before enjoyed credit services. Thus from March 1953 to June 1954 the state bank extended credits to agrarian reform beneficiaries, and to some small producers already existing before the reform, for a total of 11,881,431.50 quetzales to finance production.

At the outset the agrarian reform produced less commotion than had been expected. This was due partly to the landlords' incapacity to combat it and defend their interests, and partly to their acceptance of the reform as not too onerous. In fact, with respect to private property, the Agrarian Reform Law aimed rather at eliminating the big feudal-type farms, where vast areas of land lay idle, but respected properties of any size which were well worked. However, as will be seen below, various clauses of the law formulated exceptions to this general aim, and this was what inspired landlords' protests. Yet in practice the execution of the reform was politicalized, eventually setting off a violent reaction.

In the first place, it was possible to expropriate lands which had already been given to tenant farmers as gifts; this roused big protests from farm owners, since such lands were generally not a single unit, but scattered throughout the cultivated area; giving them to other owners meant breaking up the farms and interspersing them with many small holdings, which would have created tremendous problems for the owner of the farm. Furthermore, this clause tended to punish more severely those landowners who had given greater or lesser amounts of land to their tenants.

In the second place, the law stipulated that any population center within a farm, consisting of more than fifteen families, would be expropriated and declared an urban center. This provoked many objections by landlords, since again it broke the unity of the farms, which often contained groups of houses in the middle of them.

Another important objection to the Agrarian Reform Law was that it was unconstitutional, since leaving final decisions in the President's hands, without the right of *amparo*, contravened the separation of executive and judicial powers established in the Constitution. The seriousness of this contravention was confirmed when four Supreme Court judges were dismissed and replaced by others, for having ruled the suspension of the law's application until it was more carefully studied.

Along with this provision there was another which ruled the total expropriation, without indemnity, of lands belonging to those who opposed the Reform Law by violent or subversive means. This made it seem to landlords that they were being left no possibility of protesting, in the event that they were in disagreement over treatment received.

Obviously, another ground for protest by the landlords was the price stipulated by the law for expropriable lands; that is, the declared value for internal tax purposes, which in Guatemala was extremely low. In fact land taxes were paid on valuations which had not been adjusted since 1931, and which at that time were already low.

Landlords also objected to the composition of the local committees, which, as we have seen, were the ones recommending expropriations. These committees had five members, two named by the government and three by the local peasant union; that implied favoritism toward candidates for lands and, since there was no recourse to *amparo*, the landlords maintained it would not be possible for them to obtain impartial treatment.

Finally, since in practice under the agrarian reform program most of the land was given to peasants on a lifetime usufruct basis, instead of deeding it to them, the whole program was highly criticized as a government device to dominate the peasantry rather than to help them. To some circles in the country the political implications of this maneuver seemed extremely grave for the established order.

To the above factors was added the active political agitation and the fact that lands were distributed for proselytizing purposes, instead of on the fairest socio-economic grounds. In consequence, violent disputes began between tenant farmers and seasonal workers, between members of cooperatives and small proprietors, and between peasants of one area and others newly arrived there. All this culminated in illegal occupation of lands not subject to the law, without the authorities being able or willing to oppose it. Furthermore, at the government level there was a strong infiltration of extremist elements who, by hurrying the reform too fast for political ends, jeopardized its success.

In July 1954 the Government of Colonel Arbenz was overthrown by an armed movement led by Colonel Castillo Armas, who assumed power. Immediately the Constitution of the Republic and the Agrarian Reform Law were suspended, thus ending the above-described period of reforms (1944–1954). . . .

All the gains achieved under the Arbenz agrarian reform program were virtually nullified.

The Rebel Armed Forces (FAR)
Break with the Communists (PGT)

*Statement made by César Montes, Com-
mander in Chief of the FAR**

AT AN ESPECIALLY critical moment for the Guatemalan Revolution, at a time when the civil war is most intense and when the
internal crisis in the revolutionary movement has reached its
climax, our comrades, Major Camilo Sánchez, Captain Pablo
Monsanto, Captain Socorro Sical, Lt. Androcles Hernández
and Lt. Ramiro Díaz, guerrilla leaders of the Edgar Ibarra
Front and of the Resistance of the Central Zone, have, in the
name of the Rebel Armed Forces (FAR), taken on the historic
responsibility of publicly breaking all organic and ideological
connections with the Guatemalan Labor Party (PGT) and
have established the FAR command as an independent, centralized organism. This necessary and profoundly revolutionary
measure will be decisive in determining the prospects and
future development of the revolutionary war the people of
Guatemala are waging against their oppressors. This measure
is in line with the best tradition of the Edgar Ibarra Guerrilla
Front (FGEI) and of the whole Guatemalan guerrilla movement.

Since it was impossible for me to be on the scene of these
events, I was not able to enter into the final decision on this
measure taken by my comrades, a measure I approve in every

---

* From the text published in the *Tricontinental Bulletin*, Year III, No. 26
(May, 1968), Havana, Cuba.

aspect, in all its implications. Moreover, I consider it imperative for carrying out readjustments which cannot be postponed
if we are to go beyond, once and for all, a bogged-down phase
of incipient guerrilla development. We unpardonably allowed
our revolutionary war of liberation to be sidetracked into this
phase by the incorrect, opportunist line of general orientation
laid down by a small group of old PGT leaders—who, until a
few months ago, managed to influence the revolutionary ranks
with their policy—and also by errors we ourselves committed.

By itself, this obstacle would not be enough to justify the
need for the personal statement I am making today, especially
since it involves my approval, as I have stated, of my comrades'
actions in every respect, and regardless of the consequences.
However, it is imperative to confront and cut down with a
single blow a whole campaign of speculations and slander
which has been unleashed for the purpose of sowing discord
and uncertainty. This slander has been directed against me
personally and my present position in the revolutionary movement by certain press organs at the service of imperialism, by
the chief spokesmen of our enemies, by their self-appointed
agents and by veiled enemy elements. This campaign has
already sown doubt in the minds of some friends and comrades who have unwittingly been the first victims of this confusion and slander. Now is the time when things should be
made crystal clear.

At press conferences and in a number of communiqués,
henchmen Arana Osorio and Sosa Avila have announced my
death or disappearance. The foreign news agencies working in
Guatemala have spread such news abroad. Nicaraguan newspapers announced my death last December. Meanwhile, in
Costa Rica the press and UPI have publicly announced my
arrest and my expulsion from that country. In other countries
of the continent there has been public speculation concerning
my alleged secret presence in those countries. And recently
AP, picking up its news from information given out by one of
several anti-Communist gangs operating in our country, has

circulated throughout the world the news that I had been removed from my post as head of the FAR. One need not be very discerning to perceive that the objective of such a campaign is to create mistrust, uncertainty, the sensation that the revolutionary guerrilla movement in our country is without leadership or undermined and divided by internal rivalries—in any case, incapable of recovering and going on to victory in the next confrontations, inexorably doomed to a future of paralysis and destruction. This is one of the tricks of Yankee "psychological warfare," the political complement of the anti-guerrilla strategy they are attempting to put into effect—alternating certain bits of truth with the most absurd inventions so as to create a climate of general uncertainty, discouragement and incredulity, knowing that there are still many gullible enough to give some credence to such news reports, however unbelievable and sensational they may be. The *Imparcial*, one of the mouthpieces in this campaign, has even reached the point of insinuating that there was fratricidal war among the revolutionaries.

"It would seem the revolutionaries are throwing things at each other's heads," that paper stated a few weeks ago. And now that there is an element of truth in this—our break with the PGT—we must make everything about this event crystal-clear, in order to repel, to stop cold, all speculation, all unfounded rumors, all ingenuous or irresponsible conjectures which this might give rise to, because all this will be adding grist to the same mill: that of the enemy.

The definite break that has now occurred between the FAR and what remains of the former PGT apparatus is by no means an unexpected or accidental event. It will take very few by surprise, but no one should stand aside and fail to take a stand on this matter for lack of information. And no one should choose sides mistakenly because of confusion. This break is not a clash between brothers, nor is it a fight for positions. It is the culmination of a weeding-out process that is perfectly natural in the historical development of a revolution on the advance. The need for this break was foreseen by the FGEI in its charter in October 1964 and has almost become fact several times since then.

It was a process of divergences at first, and later of dispute, between two ideas, two attitudes toward the war, toward the Revolution, toward the people, both determined by deep class roots and a historic moment. On one side there is the revolutionary idea, which sees war as the people's instrument and method for taking power into their own hands so as to liberate themselves and make their revolution: the socialist revolution. Therefore it is not subject to the fear that this may be a total war, long, bloody and generalized. This is a radical vision, revolutionary, audacious, young, dynamic. On the other side is the pseudo-revolutionary idea, which does not believe in the people's ability to take power into their own hands; which has confidence in the ability of the bourgeoisie to direct a democratic regime of state capitalism progressing peacefully, evolving tranquilly toward socialism. It is, therefore, a concept that opposes war, is wary of the possibility of winning such a war, prefers a road of successive displacements of the bourgeois factions in power until the arrival at some combination which gives the Left influence, participation in the government. Under the pressure of events and popular feeling, this concept can go so far as to accept a limited, small-scale war, static and indefinite which, in addition, it would try to use as a political argument to make the bourgeoisie recognize its right of participation in government.

This is a submissive, opportunist, fainthearted, outmoded, passive vision. The revolutionary attitude is to anticipate events so as to act in advance and give them the form the revolution demands. The pseudo-revolutionary attitude is to close one's eyes to events and keep these events from the people's eyes in the hope that, in this way, new clashes can be avoided.

This divergence and conflict has followed an intricate course in our country and caused much suffering and many setbacks.

Lives have been lost which could have been saved; battles lost which could have been won; opportunities wasted which could have been taken advantage of for the Revolution and for the people. Reason enough to put an end to this irrational, tortuous and sterile internal conflict, whose increasing bitterness is sufficient proof of the impossibility of unity or agreements between such discordant principles. If there is something which we can and should reproach ourselves for now in relation to this break which has taken place, it is precisely for not having made it before, since it was foreseen long ago that this was the way to resolve these irreconcilable internal differences in the revolutionary movement, to free the guerrilla movement from the ties that bound it. We must recognize in a spirit of self-criticism that, consciously or unconsciously, we contributed, on some occasions, to preventing this separation from taking place when it was already a need and a possibility. It has been carried out now that nothing could have prevented or avoided it save the capitulation of the revolutionaries themselves—and that is completely unthinkable

On the other hand, this break fully corresponds to a historic law which, far from being alien to the revolutionary experience of the world, has been applied, at opportune moments, by all true revolutionaries, beginning with Marx and Lenin, who did not hesitate to break with the opportunists, because, with the advance of the revolution to more bitterly contested stages, it becomes necessary to free it of the individuals, groups or currents that, incapable of facing the ever bloodier struggle, try to halt the development of the revolution and to avoid sacrifices and responsibilities. In a war process this dead weight takes a toll of innumerable lives, inflicts suffering, delays victory and causes setbacks. We're not saying this just to hear ourselves talk. We can prove what we say simply by casting a glance at the recent, short history of our revolutionary war.

It is known that not one single military operation in our armed struggle to date has been inspired, guided or led—directly or indirectly—by the leading clique of the PGT, which calls itself a party. Its members never bothered to study the problems of war or its laws; they never made any attempt to analyze the experiences gained through the people's combats; on no occasion did they even set about formulating a strategic plan for the war. How did they presume to lead a revolution whose course, as they themselves have admitted verbally, is that of war?

But there's a lot more. Some of them have said that, if they don't constitute the "practical" vanguard, they are the vanguard ideologically and politically. Let us review the happenings that, in one way or another, constitute the chain of political events that have marked the course and determined the trend of our revolutionary war.

February 6, 1962, marks the conscious beginning of the guerrilla war in our country, in the sense that it constitutes an armed struggle taking place in the countryside, counting on the political and social support of the peasants, and initiated by an irregular, rudimentary military force of limited numbers. This action, commanded by the then lieutenants Marco Antonio Yon Sosa, Luis Turcios Lima and Luis Trejo Esquivel, also established the public personality of the 13th of November Movement. Its impact on the nation made conditions ripe for the popular rebellion of March–April of that year, a profound popular shock which determined definitively the course of the Guatemalan Revolution. As we know, this rebellion, kept afloat for two months by the urban masses, without a defined leadership, without clear orientation and without adequate organization, was finally overcome by the Ydígoras regime.

In December 1962, following the initiative of the 13th of November Movement, the first FAR was established, conceived as the political-military alliance of the M-13, the PGT and the 12th of April Movement, the university contingent remaining from the March–April mobilizations.

On October 16, 1964, in the face of the split which separated the M-13—whose leadership had been seized, for the time being, by foreign Trotskyite elements—and the PGT, the Edgar Ibarra Guerrilla Front, in a letter addressed to both organizations, defined itself as a revolutionary force with its own features and with an approach that was different both militarily and politically from those of the PGT and 13th of November, from whose ranks we had emerged.

In March, 1965, after having withdrawn from the M-13, Major Luis Turcios Lima, representing the Edgar Ibarra Guerrilla Front, called a conference of the leaders of the PGT and JPT * as well as of the chiefs of the different zones of resistance, which were functioning in a more or less dislocated manner as a result of the split that had occurred in the first FAR. The Provisional Center of Revolutionary Leadership (CPDR) of the FAR emerged from this meeting, an organizational attempt which later lost its vitality and which failed to unify the revolutionary movement and to give the guerrilla movement a centralized leadership and headquarters.

In none of these events that have shaped a course and determined objective phases and advances in the still brief history of our revolutionary guerrilla war, a chain of positive features typifying our Revolution, has the initiative, foresight, inspiration or organizational contribution of the PGT leadership been present, except for the founding of the FAR and the CPDR, in which it had to participate due to the initiative of other forces; and, in any event, its contribution was to hold back and deflect the momentum and original objective, and not to stimulate and develop it. In other happenings, its absence was complete. How is it possible that the leadership of a party that defines itself as the revolutionary vanguard of the proletariat and the people in ideology and practice could be absent from the most critical revolutionary events, in which the protagonists were the popular, revolutionary and progressive forces and masses?

It has given—and will certainly continue to give—excuses

---

* The JPT (Juventud Patriótica del Trabajo), now defunct, was an organization of young workers.—*Translator*.

and justifications; but there is only one real reason. The leadership of the PGT is not guided by revolutionary concepts, and it never had a revolutionary attitude in practice. It did not give guidance, nor did it act, at the most critical, explosive and militant points of popular discontent.

However, the leadership of the PGT was present in and was the source of inspiration, directly or indirectly, and the instrument for promoting or organizing the following measures that affected the war and the Revolution in a negative way:

The formation of an electoral bloc with the Party of Revolutionary Unity (PUR): a measure that dissipated much popular energy and hopes of a revolutionary character at a point when the armed struggle was getting under way and that, in the last analysis, became a focal point of compromises and electoral dickering with sectors of the bourgeoisie and petty bourgeoisie.

The sad defeat at Concuá: tragic culmination of the armed operation that, termed a "guerrilla" action, was in reality a test of armed "pressure" intended to guarantee the participation of military elements from the liberal petty bourgeoisie in a supposed "military junta." According to calculations badly made, this "junta" would replace the Ydígoras government on its "imminent" collapse to be brought about by the March–April rebellion, the outcome of which is well known.

Electoral support of the candidacy of Jorge Toriello—a rather unpopular homegrown bourgeois Liberal politician—for Mayor of Guatemala City at the end of 1962: this was not only a distraction of the revolutionary effort still hot from the March–April rebellion, but led Toriello and the forces that supported him to a sad and predictable political defeat.

Within the Center of Revolutionary Leadership, whose fundamental practical purpose was to constitute a national and centralized command for the war, the political leaders of the PGT took the initiative to form "concentric" regional organizations of the PGT and the FAR. The practical and certainly deliberate consequence of this measure was the dispersion of forces, weapons and efforts of all kinds. The objective purpose of creating several guerrilla fronts, autonomous in practice (given the absence of a centralized command and of a joint strategy) resulted, as we know, in the ideological confrontation of these incipient focal groups with the FGEI, giving official recognition to a dispersion that has to this day had painful consequences.

The PGT National Conference's "rejuvenation" of its Central Committee with a certain number of outstanding young cadres from the guerrilla struggle or tasks related to it—with the announced intention of incorporating the entire PGT in the war—turned out simply to be a maneuver to neutralize the most radical proposals and swamp the military leaders in an involved disciplinary setup. It was not by chance that, following this conference, some international publications of European Communist Parties began speaking of the FAR as the "armed forces of the PGT."

FAR support for the candidacy of the present imperialist puppet in our country, Méndez Montenegro: this was decided on by the CPDR at the initiative of the PGT, in the absence of Major Turcios and with my vote—as representative of the FGEI—cast against it. Incidentally, the result of that vote shows how the CPDR, an instrument for constructing a centralized command of the revolutionary war, had been converted into a tool for conciliation with the bourgeoisie, in the hands of the "politicians" of the PGT leadership clique. It is not amiss here to recall what Major Turcios stated from abroad concerning those elections: "We do not propose to keep the elections from taking place, because we still are not strong enough for that and because there are still quite a few ordinary people who, misled, still place some faith in the electoral game. Therefore, the elections will take place. But let it be known that, when our forces have grown sufficiently and our people have become more aware of the spurious nature of elections when a reactionary government holds power, we will use force to prevent the continuation of this vile deception of the people." And he continued: "If we revolutionaries participate in those elections or urge the people to participate in them, voting for the PR or any other opposition party, we are giving our support, our backing in principle, our revolutionary approval and the support of the masses who believe in us, to people who we know are devoid of scruples, who we know are accomplices of reaction and imperialism."

And in the end, although there are no documents to attest to it, this same leadership clique of the PGT has also been the instigator of and intermediary for the establishment of trade relations between the Méndez Montenegro government and the socialist countries, a measure which has already been approved by the cabinet, according to a public announcement made by Foreign Minister Arenales Catalán.

This is not a measure recently conceived. It is the result of careful planning and a negotiation that began to gestate with the flamboyant inauguration of "constitutionality" with the PR in power, and that has occupied the attention and study of the leading organ of the PGT. What an astonishing duality, impossible to justify either politically or morally, when a party can conduct such negotiations at a time that its militants, and members of its own Central Committee, are being assassinated and hunted down by the repressive forces of the government: the same government whose authorization is sought so as to sanctify trade relations between the coffee-growing bourgeoisie and some socialist countries!

None of these measures, initiated, inspired or organized by or at the behest of the leadership group of the PGT, has been a positive or worthwhile contribution to the Revolution; nor have any of them brought about any progress in our war. On the contrary, they have been the desperate expression of a congenital fear of war, of revolutionary progress; they have acted as a brake, an attempt to lead the struggle into conciliation, into retreat, or at best, into a chronic guerrilla war incapable of determining anything politically—in other words, into class capitulation.

And we ask ourselves: What has this vanguard role they

proclaim consisted of? Concretely, what has been the upshot of the influence unfortunately exercised by the traditional PGT leadership group in the revolutionary war that our people are waging so relentlessly against their oppressors, their class enemies, their executioners? And our answer is: It has been of no assistance. It has been too much of an obstruction. Now it will not continue holding us back from within, and we will not allow it to do so from without.

In conclusion, the differences and conflicts that have led the FAR, the true and active revolutionaries, to break with the vestiges of the bureaucratic leadership apparatus of the PGT, involve not just a conflict between two different lines, but a struggle between two mutually exclusive tendencies in the revolutionary process: the struggle between healthy and malignant forces.

From now on, the responsibility for setbacks and victories will fall exclusively on the combatants themselves; the potential for leading, succeeding, failing, will rest directly in the hands of the guerrilla leaders. The political line, strategy and tactics are our responsibility and our task. It is up to us; we cannot escape this responsibility.

We are not starting from zero; we have a lot of experience that should help us move forward wisely; we have the tremendous combative spirit of our people; we are imbued with a just and sacred hatred of the enemy that permits us neither truce nor indecision. And we have outlined, more clearly than ever, the general lines of the strategy corresponding to warfare in our country, in our continent. If we do not triumph, we will not try to justify ourselves—we will die fighting—but we will certainly have contributed to blazing the way for those who will follow. We accept these responsibilities fully, as we accept the responsibility for having tolerated for so long the situation from which we have just emerged. Perhaps there only remains for me to make public my resignation from membership in the PGT and from all the positions in its hierarchy to which I was named. This statement will acquaint the Guatemalan people with this fact, and also comrades and friends in other countries. But I will never resign my position as a Communist, which is earned not through a membership card but through struggle, through combat, through acting ideologically in harmony with the proletariat—that is, serving its interests in every way.

Now, when imperialism is bleeding itself to death in furious desperation under the telling blows that are being meted out by the glorious Peoples' Liberation Armed Forces and heroic people of Vietnam; now, when the valiant peoples of Korea and Cuba triumphantly defy the provocations of imperialism, reiterating their readiness to confront and crush it; now, when the puppets and advisers of imperialism are biting the dust in every country where the people have risen up, shouldering arms; now, when throughout the world, even within their own country, there is a strong popular movement of protest against the Yankees; now, when unfortunately there are so many watchful, timid and opportunistic elements that frantically search for ways to placate the rage, threats and blackmail of imperialism, now is the moment for definitions and decisions. Let no one abstain from taking up his position at this time! Let no one abstain from taking his place in the war, wherever his homeland and history call him! We are followers of Major Ernesto Che Guevara, and we shall be faithful to his example, his motto and his memory.

Following the Combative Example of Major Turcios Lima, Ever Onward to Victory!

To Win or Die for Guatemala and Socialism!

CÉSAR MONTES

Commander in Chief of the FAR

January 21, 1968

The Guerrilleros Unite

*Declaration of Unification of the Rebel
Armed Forces and the 13th of November
Revolutionary Movement (MR-13)**

THE PROCESS of the struggle of the Guatemalan people and particularly the development of the revolutionary war has placed in relief a great number of new problems that the vicissitudes of combat and experiences of all kinds pose more and more as urgently requiring a correct solution. Practical problems and tactical questions, indissolubly linked to revolutionary theory and strategy, in a word, to ideology, have had to be examined again and again in order to clarify the nature and character of the discrepancies that have sometimes separated the most consistent and honest revolutionaries.

It is a well known fact that during these past years there has been a serious leadership crisis in the ranks of the armed combatants of the Guatemalan people. This crisis came essentially from the attempt to apply to present conditions methods of political work that a long tradition of activity within the organizations and framework of the Communist Party had converted into mechanical and dogmatic approaches, slow and parliamentary; in addition due to their formation and subjective conditions, influential sectors of the PGT never conceived of the people taking power, but stayed with the pure and simple conception of a proletariat converted, at best, into a force of pressure.

---

* Translated from the text published in February 1968, in the first issue of *Guerrillero*, new organ of the Rebel Armed Forces.

But also contributing to the leadership crisis was the experience the forward-moving Guatemalan revolution had with one of the four expressions of contemporary Trotskyism, as much because of the mistaken conceptions of the latter, as because its presence served as a good pretext to those interested in dividing the revolutionaries and in obstructing the progress of the struggle.

Despite the grave difficulty this crisis represented in the effort to confront the national and class enemy, the Rebel Armed Forces and the 13th of November Movement demonstrated their will to keep up the struggle and its political vitality, resisting the adversary, striking counter-blows and insisting whenever the occasion arose on the search for a new level of unity for the armed combatants.

It is inconceivable that there should continue to exist two parallel movements which affirm that armed struggle is the only road history shows our people for achieving liberty, progress and justice; which do not vacillate in proclaiming as their aim the taking of power in order to establish a revolutionary government to serve as an instrument for doing away with the cruel exploitation imperialism imposes on Guatemalan workers, peasants, the poor middle class and the country in general; which, with genuine proletarian realism, consider that solidarity among peoples who fight for progress and against all subjection, ceases to be literary only when one struggles nationally. That is, in this hour of the world, real solidarity among combatants is achieved attacking and destroying imperialism and its oligarchical allies within national limits.

Only with unity is it possible to concentrate the resources of war and lead the people to victory. Sporadic, isolated actions and even the most harmonious cooperation are limited in comparison with organic unity, with total integration in a single structure. Besides, the form of struggle that has been imposed on us demands of us an iron discipline and a vertical hierarchy. And this can only be achieved with the organic unity of all armed combatants.

In the long and difficult road that the leaders of the *Rebel Armed Forces and the 13th of November Revolutionary Movement* have traveled to achieve unity, there stand out: the famous judgment against the Trotskyites in the "Alejandro de León" Guerrilla Front, which culminated with the expulsion of the four last Trotskyite elements that remained in the ranks of MR-13; the visit that Comandante César Montes made to the "Alejandro de León" Guerrilla Front in mid-1966; the visit that Comandante Marco Antonio Yon Sosa made to the "Edgar Ibarra" Guerrilla Front in October of the same year; the independence obtained by the FAR on liberating itself from the dogmatic tutelage of the opportunistic coterie of the PGT, and finally the sustained revolutionary debates held at the end of January of this year between the FAR and MR-13, and which concluded with *the following agreements*:

FIRST: The total and definitive integration of the Rebel Armed Forces and the 13th of November Revolutionary Movement, in a single organization that will be named *Rebel Armed Forces*.

SECOND: The integration of a *single command*, whose members, in order are Comandantes *Marco Antonio Yon Sosa* and *César Montes*.

THIRD: The adoption of the same politico-military line and the same strategic conception in the development of the Revolutionary War.

The definitive and total unification of the consistently revolutionary forces, of the fighting vanguard of the workers, peasants, and all Guatemalan people, strengthens the revolutionary movement in our country. This reality, by itself alone, is a serious setback for the anti-patriotic and retrograde forces who serve the bloody puppet government of President Méndez Montenegro.

The great importance of these agreements reached in such historic meetings, the real advance that this unification represents, explains why the contents of the agreements should be immediately made known to all our combatants, as well as to our sympathizers, friends and revolutionaries in general, so that they may take the corresponding measures and that, as soon as possible, *this agreed-upon organic unification will be projected to all places and levels.* At the same time *they should study and apply the most daring and quick methods that will consolidate the organization and give it form, leaving aside those forms of work which by their slowness and bureaucracy are inadequate and insufficient in present conditions.*

Our decision to fight until victory for the liberation of Guatemala from imperialism, for the abolition of the exploitation of the majority, for the disappearance of the injustice and arbitrariness with which the worker and peasant masses are treated, for the real implantation of democracy in our country—a decision that from now on will be more effective in practice thanks to our unity—is the fighting solidarity that we offer to all the peoples of the world who struggle for their liberation, in particular to the heroic people of Vietnam, whose battles inspire us and show us the victorious path of armed struggle.

For the sake of the most precious interests of the working people of Guatemala, of the peasants, of the other exploited sectors, at the same time that we communicate our unification, we repeat our firm, unbreakable decision to

WIN OR DIE FOR GUATEMALA

Marco Antonio Yon Sosa
César Montes

Sierra de las Minas
Guatemala
February, 1968

Revolution Is Guatemala's Only Solution

> *Statement by Father Thomas Melville, suspended as a priest of the Maryknoll order and asked to leave Guatemala after his guerrilla connections became known to his religious superiors.**

MISERY IS perhaps the biggest factor in preventing a true growth of Christianity in Latin America today, as it would be anyplace else.

Misery is that state in which a man lacks a sufficient supply of life's very essentials so that his total energies are engaged in a constant struggle with nature. He continually experiences hunger; his home is often made of reject materials on land not his own; his bathing and toilet facilities are shared with the animal kingdom; and the lack of opportunity for any decent type of education leaves him bewildered before all encounters with the challenge of nature.

His life is one of perpetual struggle to stay alive, and any hope to develop within him a real concern for his fellow man borders on the cynical.

Misery must not be confused with poverty, a Christian virtue or condition which satisfies man's basic needs and is willing to forgo life's superfluities. Thus misery, which is the lack of these basics, makes the practice of Christian love physically as well as psychologically next to impossible. St. James

---

* From *The National Catholic Reporter*, January 31, 1968, copyright 1968 by *National Catholic Reporter*. Reprinted with permission.

says that a man who tells his neighbor to be clothed and filled and does nothing about it is a hypocrite. How do we expect Christianity to flourish in an environment where a man has to struggle to stay alive, where he can't even afford to feed and clothe himself, let alone his neighbor?

Today we hear community talked about on all sides: the Christian community. This is charity, love, translated into the local context. Some kind of a real physical sharing, as well as the spiritual, has to be possible; some kind of a natural community has to exist, before Christianity can be planted. There is not much room in Latin America for the masses to practice this kind of sharing as things stand now, and the possibility becomes even more remote as the misery increases in proportion to the population growth, and the greater concentration of economic power in the hands of the minority.

Could we say that the hierarchy has tried to alleviate this misery?

Wouldn't it be more true to say that they are even here guilty of a grave irresponsibility? Their insistence on preaching a legalistic Catholicism, based on rites and sacraments, without any real attempt to translate their significance into daily living, is a fact that cannot be questioned. Their reluctance even today to turn back to the people lands that are rightfully theirs has had few exceptions. Nor has their propensity for large episcopal palaces, police escorts, ring kissing and all the other trappings of temporal wealth and power.

Their unwillingness to proclaim Christ's Gospel in the face of political and economic pressures has had few, though inspiring, exceptions.

Last year, during a big "crash" mission for the whole archdiocese of Guatemala, the archbishop (Mario Casariego of Guatemala City) instructed all the preachers to overlook the theme of social justice because it was a controversial subject. On two occasions, in Guatemala and in El Salvador, rich contributors to seminary construction funds were able to silence social-minded priests by threatening their bishops with economic retaliation.

The two most progressive lay movements, the "Cursillos de Cristiandad" and the Christian Family movement, are almost exclusively the terrain of the rich, which further forges the marriage between the hierarchy and the wealthy minority. It must be kept in mind that this minority not only refuses to fulfill its obligation of alleviating the misery of the masses, but is the very cause of it.

THE ABOVE seems like a rather harsh picture of Latin American Catholicism. The reality is harsher still and any sincere observer cannot but note the same. If, then, such is the state of things, where, might we ask, is the Church in Latin America going?

There is only one road open to it: Revolution. A Revolution which will effect the complete change in structures within the body of the faithful and within the civil society where these faithful must live and act.

Evolution is no longer possible because this presupposes, or rather is, the gradual and natural growth of an organism. But the growth of Christianity has been stifled these many years, if in truth it was ever really planted, and now revolution is necessary. Revolution means a profound and abrupt change in a relatively short time, and this process has already begun, both in the Church proper and in civil society. Which will affect the other more is not really the question, because our present understanding of the Church makes us see the revolution in both, as one and the same.

Of what will the revolution consist?

As it affects the structure of the Church proper, it will mean that the hierarchy will slip back to a functional position of teaching Christ's Gospel, losing at the same time their positions of political, social and economic power. If, as individuals in the structure, they refuse to face this change, they will be discounted and will bring discredit on themselves and the doctrine they pretend to represent. They must be shown that their leadership is one of faith and charity, and not the temporal powers that they have supplanted them with. The faithful will pick their priests and bishops from among their own number, whose lives will be at one and the same time a living lesson of Christ's message and an indication of the growth in his grace of the community they represent.

We will return to the belief that the Church is infallible, and that the Holy Father is also infallible only when he acts as spokesman for the beliefs that exist in the body of the faithful. The legalisms that have reigned these many centuries— including celibacy, the so-called "glory of the priesthood of the Western Church" which is now confused with the state of non-marriage—will be replaced by the primacy of faith and charity.

But the Christian lives in a world, his world, God's world, where he must work, eat, sleep and play. It is his world and his brother's world, made up of dynamic relationships between these brothers. We have sciences that study these relationships called sociology, economics, politics. If what Christ taught has meaning, the Christian must bring his beliefs into practice in the realm of sociology, economics, and politics. If he fails to do this, his faith is in vain, as St. James says. He does this, not in the name of Christ, but in his own name because he is a Christian.

As soon as Christians in any number begin to put into practice their Christian beliefs in these fields, then Latin America will positively experience a Revolution. This is as certain as the fact that the present socio-economic and political makeup of Latin America is not just unchristian but anti-Christian.

Its society is composed of such sharp and pitiful class distinctions, that many have reached the level of despair so as to believe that their misery, sickness and ignorance are a punishment from God for past and long forgotten sins, while the

rich believe that their wealth is an indication of God's blessing and predestination to salvation.

Its economic institutions are still completely "laissez faire"
capitalism, which we prefer to think died out in the first
decades of this century. Any capitalist system, whether it be
"laissez faire" or not, is based essentially on competition,
rugged individualism, the profit motive, and it is difficult to
see how such a system, though materially successful, can ever
be supported by a Christian society that truly understands
Christ's message of love.

Politically, Latin America is rated among the free nations
of the world, but political freedom, as is all freedom, is in
direct proportion to the education and culture of the person
exercising that freedom. This, in itself, is not enough, but it
is the necessary beginning; and we need not cite Latin American educational statistics to show that it is almost completely
lacking among her masses.

So what is left open to her? It is obvious: revolution. She
cannot wait for an evolutionary process to heal these ills. These
ills have been festering too long, and are now too far advanced
for the strength of the organism to combat and heal them.
Surgery is necessary. This is the common opinion of the most
serious students of the Latin American scene.

THE REAL question is not: Whether or not the revolution? but
rather: the revolution, peaceful or violent?

As Christians, we cannot but desire the peaceful change, the
peaceful process. Christ came to bring us peace, and man by
nature wants peace for himself if not for his fellow man.

But true peace is the result of justice, as the Holy Father
says, and justice is the reciprocal relationship between two
beings or groups where each recognizes the basic rights of the
other.

The revolution can only be peaceful when those who control the structures, the rich oligarchy, are willing to allow such

a change to occur, recognizing the long-denied rights of the poor masses. To the degree that they oppose such a change, the masses will be forced to use ever more drastic measures, to take the power into their own hands and thus effect the change by themselves.

It is the rich then, with those of allied interests, who have the real say as to whether the process will be peaceful or violent. "Those who make pacific revolution impossible, make violent revolution inevitable" (JFK). We have only to ask them, what is the answer of the rich to the demand of the poor for their human rights? Will they allow it to be peaceful or will they oppose it with all the means at their disposal? It is only left for us now to examine the present and recent past of the Latin American power structure to see what alternative they have already picked.

Guatemala is a good case in point. I have worked there these past 10 years, as a priest of the Maryknoll order and can talk with some authority.

In recent weeks, Guatemala has been in the world's news because of a series of killings, which the press calls a series of vindictive measures on the part of the right and left wing extremists. Meanwhile the government supposedly maintains the position of left-center while trying to crush the violence on both sides.

This is simply not true. The government almost openly supports the rightist groups and many of their members hold high positions in it.

The National Liberation Movement (MLN) which was started by assassinated president Castillo Armas and is still his heir, makes no bones about the fact that it controls the rightist terrorists called the "Mano Blanca" (White Hand). NOA (New Anti-communist Organization), another band of terrorists on the right, is headed by Colonel of the Army Maximo Zepeda Martínez and Lieutenant Hugo Edmundo Alonzo and Luis Dominguez, all on active duty. The headquarters of the "Mano Blanca" is in the main police building in downtown Guatemala. A common joke in the capital is that the Minister of Defense, Colonel Arriaga Bosque, is the real president and not Julio César Méndez Montenegro. Even if this were not true, anyone acquainted with Latin American politics knows that the president can't lift a finger without the permission of the army chiefs. The third rightist terrorist group, CADEG, is composed of ruffians paid by the rich landowners to "take care" of any "troublemakers." This, of course, includes anyone who begins protesting too loudly about the injustices of the actual situation.

During the past 18 months, these three groups together have assassinated more than 2,800 intellectuals, students, labor leaders and peasants who have in any way tried to organize and combat the ills of Guatemalan society. The "Mano Blanca" itself admits that not more than one in ten of these is probably a communist.

I personally know a good friend and benefactor of the Maryknoll Fathers, a daily communicant, who accused a Christian labor leader who was trying to organize a union on his big sugar plantation of communism and thus had him shot by the army. This man today, like many other landowners, maintains army guards on his farm to avoid the repetition of such an occurrence in the future.

When the cooperative I started among the destitute Indians of Quezaltenango was finally capable of buying its own truck, the rich tried to pay off the driver to run the vehicle off a cliff. When the truck driver wouldn't be bought, at least four attempts were made to run it off the road, one of them successful.

In the parish of San Antonio Huista, where my brother, also a Maryknoll priest, was pastor, the president of a land cooperative was killed by the town's wealthy, including the mayor. When the case went to the Huehuetenango capital, the judge had already been bought off and nothing could be done about it.

The three leaders of the parish cooperative in La Libertad,

Huehuetenango, have also been accused of communism and threatened with death because of their efforts to elevate their neighbors.

I could go on and on with a list that would fill a book, but the point is: The oligarchy and the army control and *are* the government.

They will also go to any lengths to prevent the peasant from elevating himself to a point where he has any real economic or political power. He works now for 80 cents a day while the rich make and bank millions from his sweat. He will be allowed to improve if it's simply a question of putting in toilets or digging wells, but anything that would alter the oligarchy's life-and-death control over him will be resisted with the worst of viciousness.

In a situation such as outlined above, what is the peasant to do? He can do one of two things: he can surrender to the pressures to keep him down, and thus renounce his humanity; or he can protest, grab a gun and defend himself, his family and his neighbors. He has chosen the first road for the most part until recently, but there are now indications that he will not do so much longer.

AND WHERE does the hierarchy stand on all this? Last year the bishops of Guatemala came out with a pastoral letter denouncing the violence and calling on both sides to talk out their differences. It's like asking God and the devil to come to some kind of agreement, and the result was just what could have been expected: nothing.

Recently, the archbishop, in the face of criticism for his weekly sermon to the poor to conform themselves to their lot, declared that henceforth his birthday would be a "Day for the Poor" and that he would be known as "the Archbishop of the Poor." On this day he gives out surplus food and old clothing to the people that come begging to his door. Some are still wondering what happens to them the other 364 days of the year.

In a meeting a few months ago of the peasant leaders in La Democracia, Huehuetenango, the Maryknoll superior of Guatemala told the assembled group that Christ said: "The poor you will always have with you," so that they had better conform themselves to their misery and not be agitating for change.

When 25 priests assembled to try to organize the agricultural workers on the big farms on the South Coast, the bishops of Huehuetenango (an American)* San Marcos (a Spaniard); Quezaltenango (a Spaniard), and Solola (an Italian) wrote all of us involved a strong letter forbidding us to take part, stating that it was none of our business and that we should content ourselves with preaching the gospel.

Many of us have been pleased at the attention that Latin America received from John Kennedy and Pope John, but not with the results. And what are these results? Simply that the old order of injustice and tyranny has been strengthened and not weakened by this interest.

The U.S. government has sent jets, helicopters, weapons, money and military advisers to the government that only strengthens its control over the peasant masses. This past year, 1967, salaries, uniforms, arms and vehicles for 2,000 new policemen were paid for by the Alliance for Progress. This year another 1,500 are projected for enlistment, to say nothing about the secret intelligence services rendered for ferreting out all "social disturbers."

The U.S. Church also contributes to this aggravating situation: building fine rectories, convents, schools and churches throughout Latin America, distributing all kinds of food, medicine, and clothing that only succeed in temporarily quieting the restlessness of the less foresighted. U.S. churchmen strengthen the already decaying hierarchical structure by building seminaries (that will soon be empty), by aiding the

---

* The Maryknoll headquarters identified him as Bishop Hugo Gerbermann, a member of their order.—*Editor.*

Latin bishops to organize themselves on diocesan and national levels, which only tighten their social and economic control over the people.

For the money and the personnel that they receive from the U.S., many in Latin America are willing to sacrifice all vestiges of the national identity of their flocks in order to make them little U.S. ghettos.

The head of the national secretariat of the bishops of Guatemala is an American. The head of the drive for the new national major seminary is an American. The reason: money and personnel. The Guatemalan clergy can hardly protest but the hard feelings created among them are clearly evident.

HAVING COME to the conclusion that the actual state of violence, composed of the malnutrition, ignorance, sickness and hunger of the vast majority of the Guatemalan population, is the direct result of a capitalist system that makes the defenseless Indian compete against the powerful and well-armed landowner, my brother and I decided not to be silent accomplices of the mass murder that this system generates.

We began teaching the Indians that no one will defend their rights, if they do not defend them themselves. If the government and oligarchy are using arms to maintain them in their position of misery, then they have the obligation to take up arms and defend their God-given right to be men.

We were accused of being communists along with the people who listened to us, and were asked to leave the country by our religious superiors and the U.S. ambassador. We did so.

But I say here that I am a communist only if Christ was a communist. I did what I did and will continue to do so because of the teachings of Christ and not because of Marx or Lenin. And I say here too, that we are many more than the hierarchy and the U.S. government think.

When the fight breaks out more in the open, let the world

know that we do it not for Russia, not for China, nor any other country, but for Guatemala. Our reponse to the present situation is not because we have read either Marx or Lenin, but because we have read the New Testament.